Essays & Studies
1984

Collected by
Raymond Chapman

JOHN MURRAY, LONDON
HUMANITIES PRESS, ATLANTIC HIGHLANDS, N.J.

ESSAYS AND STUDIES 1984
IS VOLUME THIRTY-SEVEN IN THE NEW SERIES
OF ESSAYS AND STUDIES COLLECTED ON BEHALF OF
THE ENGLISH ASSOCIATION

© The English Association 1984

First published 1984
by John Murray (Publishers) Ltd
50 Albemarle Street, London W1X 4BD

Typeset by Fakenham Photosetting Ltd, Fakenham, Norfolk
Printed and bound in Great Britain at
The Pitman Press, Bath

British Library Cataloguing in Publication Data

Essays and studies.—1984
1. English literature—History and criticism—Periodicals
820.9   PR13

ISBN 0–7195–4133–6

Humanities Press ISBN 0–391–03059–0

Preface

A volume of literary essays published in 1984 might perhaps be expected to take the form of tributes to George Orwell, or studies of futuristic and dystopic fantasies. Dates arrive, are celebrated and forgotten, while English literature continues its thousand years of development. This volume has no single theme, but collections tend to reflect the interest of their editors: a number of papers dealing with the Victorian period or with the connections between literature and theology is not fortuitous. There is, however, a wide spread of interest: from Old English to a theme in which reference is made to Allen Ginsberg.

The English Association is concerned with all aspects of English language and literature, past, present and to come. Like its predecessors, this number of *Essays and Studies* is intended to give pleasure as well as, it is hoped, making some contribution to the ever-growing output of scholarship. Personal appreciation increased by the insights of other readers is a proper aim of the Association and its publications.

It may be that whatever helps to preserve our literary heritage and to ensure its transmission to another generation is a small but not negligible contribution to the avoidance of telescreens and Newspeak.

Raymond Chapman

Contents

Illustrations

I

Time and the Passing of Time in 'The Wanderer' and Related OE Texts

JANET BATELY

The Anglo Saxons, like us, divided time up into years, months, weeks, days and hours. Like us, they subdivided years into seasons, and days into nights and days.[1] Like ours their grammatical structures and lexis allowed them to determine and define the temporal relationship between events and to indicate not only the time of an action but also its quality or manner. However, in a number of ways their perception of time and the passing of time differed from ours, partly for religious and philosophical reasons, partly because of limited technical and historical[2] knowledge, partly because of differences in syntax or lexis. Thus, just as for the Romans the *hora* was of varying length according to the time of year, the period from sunrise to sunset being reckoned as twelve hours, so initially for the Anglo-Saxons a winter's hour was by definition shorter than a summer one. As King Alfred says in his rendering of Boethius, *De Consolatione Philosophiae*, God gives short hours to winter days, longer ones to those of summer (10.10–11), a statement which he expands in his metrical version:

> hwæt ðu, fæder, wercest
> sumurlange dagas   swiðe hate;
> þæm winterdagum   wundrum sceorta
> tida getiohhast   (Met. 4.18–21).[3]

[1] See F. Tupper, 'Anglo-Saxon Dæg-mæl', *PMLA*, 10 (1895), pp. 111–241.

[2] For the handling of history in some OE texts of the late ninth century, see *The OE Orosius*, ed. Janet Bately (Oxford, 1980) and idem, 'World History in the *Anglo-Saxon Chronicle*: its sources and its separateness from the OE Orosius', *Anglo-Saxon England*, 8 (1979), pp. 177–94. Since the Bible was a major source of historical knowledge, the possibility of reading and interpreting the scriptures in more than one way necessarily coloured the Anglo-Saxons' perception of history as a whole.

[3] *King Alfred's Old English Version of Boethius De Consolatione Philosophiae*, ed. W.J. Sedgefield (Oxford, 1899). For an 'hour' of fixed length see the OE Martyrology, May 31, and Bede, *Ecclesiastical History of the English People*, ed. B. Colgrave and R.A.B. Mynors (Oxford, 1969), p. 17.

The term *winter* could be used then as now of the season, function-
ing either as the antonym of summer or as part of the lexical set
lencten, sumor, hærfest, winter, or it could be used interchangeably
with *gear* to delineate a twelve month period or 'year'.[4] *Niht* similarly
could either function as the antonym of *dæg,* or be used interchangeably with it to refer to the 'civil' day of 24 hours. At a grammatical
level, although Old English had developed a range of periphrasic
verb forms, these merely served to supplement an older binary
system of tenses, which was more widely and more freely used than
its modern equivalent. And perhaps most significant of all, the
Anglo-Saxons appear to have seen time as something inseparable
from the existence of the world, which for them was not our small
and minor planet Earth, part of the solar system, but the centre of the
universe. The world, they believed, would last 6000 years from the
day of its creation, a single act which they dated approximately
5196 BC.[5] Both it and the heavens would very shortly cease to exist,
on a day already determined by God but not precisely known to
man, human kind then proceeding to either an everlasting heaven or
an equally eternal hell.[6] So for the Anglo-Saxons what may be
termed linear time was strictly finite, encapsulated in eternity.
Moreover, what for a man was divisible into past, present, and future
was for God all present. As Alfred observes: *þæt an us is gewislice
andweard þæt þe þonne bið; ac him is eall andweard, ge þætte ær wæs, ge
þætte nu is, ge þætte æfter us bið: eall þæt is him andweard (Alfred's
Boethius* 148.10–12). So the complex relationship between God and
man, this world and eternity, meant that linear time was only one
way of looking at events in this world, to be set alongside other types
of time, such as cyclical time and the figural time of Biblical
exegesis.[7] What might seem from one standpoint a very long time
indeed was, viewed from another, but a moment, a mere twinkling
of an eye, as the Old English Bede puts it, likening the present life of
man on earth to the passage of a sparrow through a hall in winter,

---

[4] See Bede's comment on *winterfylleþ, Opera de Temporibus,* ed. C.W.
Jones (Cambridge, Mass., 1943), p. 212 and, for *winter* translating Latin *annus*
in dates, *The OE Orosius,* passim.
[5] See Bately, 'World History', pp. 192–4.
[6] See Vulgate, 2 Peter 3.10, *The Homilies of Wulfstan,* ed. D. Bethurum
(Oxford, 1957), pp. 212 and 155, and Ælfric, *The Homilies of the Anglo-Saxon
Church: The First Part containing the Sermones Catholici or Homilies of Ælfric,* ed.
B. Thorpe (London, 1844), I, p. 28.
[7] For the 'import' of such details as the number of months in the year and
hours in the day see Ælfric, *CH* I, p. 396.

'Hwæt he on þa tid, þe he inne bi∂, ne bi∂ hrinen mid þy storme þæs wintres; ac *þæt bi∂ an eagan bryhtm 7 þæt læsste fæc*,[8] ac he sona of wintra on þone winter eft cyme∂. Swa þonne þis monna lif to medmiclum fæce ætywe∂.' At the same time an apparently unique event could be seen to be part of a recurrent pattern: 'Just as day and night change', says King Alfred in the Soliloquies, 'so do all created things', and he adds to his source the comment that although the seasons replace each other and return so that each of them is as it was before, certain created things do not return in this way, but are just as regularly replaced by others:

Ac cuma∂ o∂re for hy, swa swa leaf on treowum; and æpla, (and) gears, and wyrtan, and trwowu foraldia∂ and forseria∂; and cuma∂ o∂∂er, grenu wexa∂, and gearwa∂, and ripa∂, for þat hy eft onginna∂ searian; and swa eall nytenu and fuge las, swelces ∂e nu ys lang æall to arimanne.[9]

'Men's bodies too grow old', he continues, 'but when they arise at doom's day the resurrected bodies will never after either end or grow old.' The end of this world and of linear time was simultaneously a new beginning, a shift to eternity—to be feared but also to be welcomed and longed for by the righteous soul.[10]

The paradoxes and potential ambiguities in the Anglo-Saxons' perception of time offered rich opportunities to their poets, as can be illustrated from one group of poems in particular, four short pieces which are often somewhat misleadingly called elegies: *The Wanderer, The Seafarer, The Ruin* and *The Wife's Lament*.[11] These poems have a particular concern with the relationship between time present, time

---

[8] *The OE Version of Bede's Ecclesiastical History of the English People*, ed. Thomas Miller, EETS, os 95, 96, 110, 111 (London, 1890–8), p. 136. The corresponding Latin refers to *paruissimo spatio serenitatis ad momentum excurso'*. See also *Alfred's Boethius* 44.11–24.

[9] *King Alfred's Version of St Augustine's 'Soliloquies'*, ed. T. Carnicelli (Cambridge, Mass., 1969), p. 53. Alfred may have derived part of this additional material from Boethius, who often uses cyclical changes of plants to illustrate God's control of the created world: see also *Alfred's Boethius* 57.32–58 and Carnicelli, p. 100.

[10] See further below, p. 12, n. 33.

[11] See *The Wanderer*, ed. T.P. Dunning and A.J. Bliss (London, 1969), *The Seafarer*, ed. I.L. Gordon (London, 1960) and *Three Old English Elegies*, ed. R.F. Leslie (Manchester, 1961). It is not possible here to discuss at length or even refer to more than a handful of the numerous interpretations of and comments on these poems.

past, and time future, and, at least in the first two named,[12] also with
the relationship between this finite world and eternity.

A number of features are common to most or all of the poems in
the group, as the use of first person 'I', creating a fixed present
stand-point,[13] and a contrast between this present stand-point, *nu*,
'now', and other times, almost exclusively in the past. And often it is
the distant past that is invoked, through use of adverbial constructions such as *iu, on ærdagum,* while in contrast to the practice in the
longer narrative poems concentration is not on fixed points of time
but on extended periods or recurrent events, expressed through such
words as *oft, hwilum* and *longe,* also *a, no, (n)æfre* and *awa* (used in
both temporal and eternal contexts) and phrases like *swiþe geneahhe*
and *ealra dogra gehwam.* Terms with precise time-reference, such as
those for specific seasons or times of day, are used not to signpost the
progress of the action but to give poetic and dramatic expression to
discomfort or anguish. Thus, the early morning, the period before
dawn, is exploited as a time of special misery.[14] Just as it is *on uhtan*
that the results of Grendel's *guðcræft* become revealed (*Beowulf* 126),
that dragons fly abroad and wreak havoc (*Beowulf* 2271 and 2760)
and that the wind from the east rises in Hell (*Genesis* 315), so it is *on
uhtan* that the woman in *The Wife's Lament* suffers *uhtceare* (1.7) and
goes *ana* 'alone' under her oak-tree, and the speaker in *The Wanderer,*
also *ana,* must lament his wretched state. The season of winter, with
its associated snow and freezing cold, is exploited in *The Wanderer*
and *The Seafarer,* in both cases with reference also to another cyclical
time division, night. And it is the accompanying distinctive feature
of night, darkness, that is of special significance. The narrator in *The
Seafarer* tells of *nearo nihtwaco,* anxious night-watches, at the prow of
his ship, of spending the entire winter on the ice-cold sea. The theme
of night and wintry weather is repeated, when the poet refers to the
shadow of night darkening and snow falling from the north:

Nap nihtscua,   norþan sniwde   (1.31)

---

[12] For a figural interpretation of *The Wife's Lament* and for *The Ruin* as a
didactic poem see, e.g., *Anglo-Saxon Poetry,* trans. and ed. S.J. Bredley
(London, 1982).

[13] In all except *The Ruin.*

[14] See E.G. Stanley, 'Old English Poetic Diction and the interpretation of
The Wanderer, The Seafarer, and *The Penitent's Prayer',* *Anglia,* 73 (1955), pp.
434–5, and J.L. Rosier, 'The Literal–Figurative Identity of the Wanderer',
PMLA, 79 (1964), p. 368, n. 9.

In *The Wanderer* too the topoi of winter and night are associated, with similar terminology. Here the speaker, like the narrator in *The Seafarer*, relates how he has experienced the miseries of the rime-cold sea and has travelled *wintercearig* over the waves. Later in the poem we are given a picture of a dreamer waking from a vision of what may be assumed to be the warmth and security of a hall to see hail and snow fall, and the final speech in the poem not only refers to snowstorms and *wintres woma*, 'terror of winter', but echoes the words of *The Seafarer* in an allusion to the deepening of the shadow of night, *nipeð nihtscua*. However, as we shall see, darkness and night play a more central role here than in *The Seafarer*.

In *The Wanderer*, winter is the only season referred to: significantly, the term *winter* is even used in preference to the neutral *gear* when the speaker states that a man cannot be truly wise before he has lived a large number of years in this world,

> *ær he age*
> *wintra dæl in woruldrice*　　　　　　　　(11.64–5).

In *The Seafarer*, however, winter is contrasted with summer, or the approach of summer,[15] with groves coming into blossom and the cuckoo uttering its mournful note:

> Bearwas blostmum nimað,　byrig fægriaþ,
> wongas wlitigað,　woruld onetteð
> . . . .
> Swylce geac monað　geomran reorde,
> singeð sumeres weard,　sorge beodeð
> bitter' in breosthord　　　　　　　　(11.48–55).

The apparent contradictory notes in this section are best resolved if we interpret it as merging cyclical time, with its recurrent seasons,

---

[15] Although modern critics often write of the approach of spring in this context (e.g. N.D. Isaacs, *Structural Principles in Old English Poetry* (Tennessee, 1968), pp. 28–9), that term is never used in the poem. However, in spite of this and in spite of different fashions in computation in the OE period, a new year is almost certainly meant here: see Ælfric, *CH* I, p. 100, where March 21st is given as the most appropriate date for the first day of the year: 'The earth also makes known by her plants, which then return to life, that the time at which they were created is the most correct beginning of the year'. Summer begins at Easter according to the binary system, on 9 May according to the division into four seasons.

and linear time, which must culminate in death for the individual or the end of the world for mankind. The cuckoo is a migrant, traditionally appearing in April and departing again in August—a fleeting visitor like Bede's sparrow, temporarily inhabiting the summer countryside just as man temporarily inhabits this world. And each start to a new cycle of the seasons, each return of the cuckoo, brings the end of the world one year closer.[16]

In *The Wife's Lament*, in contrast, summer is exploited for its long days, with the woman complaining that she must sit weeping under her oak-tree *sumorlangne dæg*. We may compare Satan's wish to escape from his fetters in hell for just an hour—a short winter's hour:

> Wa la! ahte ic minra handa geweald,
> and moste ane tid   ute weorðan,
> wesan ane winterstunde...   (*Genesis* 368–70)[17]

In their use of the topoi of winter, summer, early morning and night, this group of poems is not unique, except perhaps for the special prominence it gives to them.[18] However, the poet of *The Wanderer*, through an act of imaginative creation, moves beyond the conventional and the expected:

> Hu seo þrag gewat,
> Genap under nihthelm,   swa heo no wære!   (11.95–6)

Darkness is a significant recurrent theme in this poem. Apart from its use in its most usual literal context with reference to night-fall (11.102–4), it is referred to metaphorically in connection with the life of men and the mind in a context of meditation on this world, and apparently both literally and metaphorically of the grave. Thus, the darkness (*heolster*) of earth is said to have covered the Wanderer's lord

---

[16] See the comments on *onettan* by J.E. Cross, 'On the Allegory in *The Seafarer*', *Medium Ævum*, 28 (1959), pp. 104–5, and G.V. Smithers, 'The Meaning of *The Seafarer* and *The Wanderer*', ibid, p. 7. However, there may be a second strand of symbolism here: see *Alfred's Boethius* 52.4–5 'smylte weder bið þy þancwyrðre gif hit hwene ær bið stearce stormas 7 norðanwindas 7 micle renas 7 snawas... swa bið eac micle þe winsumre sio soðe gesælð to habbenne efter þam eormðum þisses andweardan lifes', and Ælfric, *CH* I, p. 614, 11.28–30.

[17] Cf. *Juliana* 495 *sumerlonge dæg*, where *sumerlonge* is again used to indicate maximum length of time.

[18] The term *morgen* is never found, although it occurs elsewhere in 'elegiac' contexts: cf. *morgenseoc*, *Resignation* 96; *morgenceald*, *Beowulf* 3022.

(1.23); the speaker can think of no reason in the world why his mind should not[19] grow dark when he considers the life of men—

> For þon ic geþencan ne mæg   geond þas woruld
> for hwan modsefa   min ne gesweorce,
> þonne ic eorla lif   eal geondþence   (11.58–60)

and the final speech on the subject of transience is put in the mouth of one who has wisely considered this foundation and thinks deeply about *þis deorce lif* (1.89), with this earthly life implicitly contrasted with the heavenly one, where there is eternal light.[20]

In lines 95–6, quoted above, the poet, starting from the convention that night functions in cyclical time in alternation with day, marked by the onset of darkness, and combining it with the established metaphor of time 'going' or 'passing',[21] has taken advantage of the use of the concepts 'darkness' and 'night' in Biblical imagery and their figural applications in Christian literature.[22] We may compare the Old English poem *Judith*, where the evil Holofernes so plies his doomed guests and himself with wine throughout the day that they finally lie in a drunken stupor resembling death, and night comes:

> Swa se inwidda   ofer ealne dæg
> dryhtguman sine   drencte mid wine,
> swiðmod sinces brytta,   oð þæt hie on swiman lagon,
> oferdrencte his duguðe ealle,   swylce hie wæron deaðe
>   geslegene,
> agotene, goda gehwylces.   Swa het se gumena baldor
> fylgan fletsittendum,   oð þæt fira bearnum
> nealæhte   niht seo þystre.   (11.28–34)[23]

The language the poet uses to describe the coming of night is appropriate both to temporal, and to spiritual, and to eternal darkness, a fact which is brought home to the alert reader by the verbal and syntactical parallelisms of the three main clauses, with their

[19] Or 'does not'.

[20] Cf. Ælfric, *CH* I, p. 158 'let us pray to our Lord for light: not for that light which will be ended, which will be driven away by the night ... but let us pray for that light which we can see with angels only, which shall never be ended'; also ibid, p. 144 'He is soð leoht þe todræfde þa þeostra ðises lifes'.

[21] See, e.g. *Beowulf* 210 *fyrst forð gewat, Seafarer* 80 *dagas sind gewitene*.

[22] See e.g., Isaiah 42.7; Joel 2.2; John 8.12; 12.35; I Thess. 5.1, 4 and 5;: II Peter; also Ælfric, *CH* I, pp. 36, 132, 144 and 248. For usage elsewhere in OE poetry, see Stanley, p. 435.

[23] *Judith*, ed. B.J. Timmer (1952, second ed., 1961).

verbs of related meaning, and the three subordinate clauses dependent on them, with the first and third both introduced by *oðþæt*, and the second amplifying the first. Afterwards the heroine brings about Holofernes' death *binnan anre nihte*, 'within a single night' (1.64), but though an abrupt and permanent end comes for him *on eorðan* he then passes to hell to be enveloped in everlasting darkness.

awa to ealdre   butan ende forð.   (11.112–21)

In *The Wanderer*, the darkness has blotted out not individuals, not mankind, but time itself.[24] And the poet not only employs great economy of expression, but having established the equation of the blotting out of the day by night and the passing of periods of time into oblivion, he then proceeds to reuse two of the three elements of his compressed statement (the collocation of *nipan* and *niht*), along with an established poetic variant of the third, in their more usual setting:

hrið hreosende   hrusan bindeð;
wintres woma   (þonne won cymeð,
nipeð, nihtscua)   norþan onsendeð
hreo hæglfare   hæleþum on andan.   (11.102–5)

However, although the subject of this particular passage is wintry weather and darkness, it none the less functions in the context of the same topos of transience (using the *Ubi sunt* theme) as the preceding section, reinforced by a reference to the ultimate destruction of the world. And both passages, together with the earlier description of a dream with its attendant hallucinations, combine to echo Isidore's comment on the transience of human kind; *quasi umbra transierunt, velut somnium evanuerunt; quaeruntur et non sunt*.[25]

If we turn to the handling not of the vocabulary but of the syntax of time, more specifically the use of the verb, we again find what appear to be marked similarities between the poems of our group, but also important differences. Syntax, it has been said, is the groundwork of the poet's art, and contributes more than superficial

[24] For the forgetting of individuals see *Alfred's Boethius* 46.27–30. See also *The Wife's Lament*, 23–4, '*Eft is þæt onhworfen;/ is nu fornumen, swa hit no wære*', transl. by Bradley, 'it is as though our friendship had never been', and cf. the various versions of the *Ubi Sunt* theme cited in J.E. Cross, '"Ubi Sunt" Passages in Old English—Sources and Relationships', *Vetenskaps-Societetens i Lund* (Årsbok, 1956), pp. 25–44 and *The Wanderer*, ed. R.F. Leslie (Manchester, 1966), pp. 18ff.

[25] Isidore, *Synonyma*, PL 83, col. 865.

direction to a text's meaning.[26] Old English linguistic usage differs in
a number of respects from that of Modern English and so for a full
appreciation of the handling of the syntax of the verb in these poems,
it is necessary first to identify the choices available to their authors.
As I have said, the OE system of tenses is a binary one, depending on
a simple opposition of past and present tense forms—indeed in
conjugation the OE verb distinguishes only these two tenses, supplemented by a range of periphrastic forms, or resolved tenses,
formed from a participle (past or present) or an infinitive together
with the verb 'to be', the verb 'to have', or one of the modal verbs.
However, the use of these supplementary forms seems to have
remained optional throughout the OE period, and simple present
and simple past are often used to express complicated temporal
relationships, frequently occurring where modern English would
require a resolved tense. Thus, for instance, the present (or non-past)
is used not only for a continuing state, but also for the passing
moment, the actual 'now', for the habitual and the universal or
timeless present, for the future and the future perfect. The past tense
is used not only for present-day preterite but also in contexts where
modern English would have 'resolved' forms. This sometimes leads
to ambiguity and to uncertainty for the modern reader, who is forced
to make a decision between two alternatives, as, for instance, in *The
Wanderer*, 11.8–9, where '*Oft ic sceolde cwiþan*' can be translated as
either 'I often had to lament' or 'I have often had to lament', with
important consequences for the interpretation of the poem as a
whole.[27] However, it also provides a basis for considerable variety of
technique and great subtlety on the part of the Anglo-Saxon poets.

Indeed, the choices available are exploited in different ways in each
of the four poems under discussion. In *The Ruin*, for instance, where
a ruined and decaying city is compared with its former glorious state,
the structure hinges on the opposition present/past, yet at the same
time the poet emphasizes the intimate links between the two. Thus,
the past tense is used both to provide a contrast with the present
situation and to account for it, while the present tense refers to the
'now' of performance and also reflects past events. The poet's technique is seen in miniature in the first two lines:

[26] See W. Nowottny, *The Language Poets Use* (London, 1962), p. 10,
S. Greenfield, *The Interpretation of Old English Poems* (London, 1972), p. 110.
[27] The most usual interpretation is 'I have had to', suggesting that the
wanderer is still full of grief; however, I prefer 'I had to', the implication
being that the man, having acquired wisdom no longer behaves in this way.

Wrætlic is þes wealstan,   wyrde gebræcon;
burgstede burston;   brosnað enta geweorc.

Here the present tense is used in the first and fourth clauses, at the beginning of the first line and the end of the second, and the past tense (which in this context can be rendered by either modern preterite or modern perfect) is sandwiched in the middle, the whole being welded together by primary and secondary alliteration (on *w* and *b*) and chiasmus. At the same time the poet exploits the fact that the 'resolved' perfect tense has as its basis a finite verb form in the present tense and that the past participle which forms its second component functions not only in this construction but also in others, occurring as part of a compound passive or as a qualifier:

Hrofas sind gehrorene,   hreorge torras,
hrungeat berofen,   hrim on lime,
scearde scurbeorge   scorene gedrorene
ældo undereotone.   Eorðgrap hafað
waldendwyrhtan,   forweorone geleorene,
heard gripe hrusan,   oþ hund cnea
werþeoda gewitan   (11.3–9).[28]

This passage of six and a half lines is composed of no more than two main clauses and one subordinate temporal clause, with the finite verb forms all in the present tense. However, the second of these could correspond to modern present, present continuous or future, and the third relates to either future or future perfect,[29] while the first two, 'are' and 'have', are verb forms which are potentially either verbal auxiliaries or main verbs. The rich and complex texture of the passage is achieved in part through the poet's varied way of handling nouns and adjectives in relation to their finite verbs, and in part through his skilful manipulation of non-finite verb forms. Thus, of the exceptionally high proportion of past participles that occur here, two form part of resolved tenses, two are in passive constructions, while the remaining three are post-modifiers. And in the first sentence the four past participles that depend on the single finite form

[28] Note also the poet's exploitation of parataxis to link verbal forms and his general avoidance of conjunctions.

[29] Leslie, *Elegies*, p. 69, rightly rules out past reference for *gewitan*. However, I do not agree that the word is infinitive with modal auxiliary understood, preferring to interpret it as present subjunctive with future or future perfect force.

of the verb 'to be', have the chiastic pattern resolved perfect (*sind gehrorene*), passive ([*sind* for *is*] *berofen*), passive ([*sind*] *scorene*) and resolved perfect ([*sind*] *gedrorene*). It should be noted that although the rhyming pairs *scorene gedrorene* and *forweorone geleorene* have identical surface structures, only in the second do the two components serve the same grammatical function, both acting as post-modifiers.

To be fully appreciated by the modern reader, the use of resolved tenses and past-participles here has to be seen in the context of their non-use or severely limited occurrence in the other poems of this group and the choices there exercised. Resolved tenses, bridging past and present, play a very small part indeed in these poems: *The Wanderer* has none at all, though a number of contexts would allow their use, while *The Seafarer* has only five instances out of 109 finite verb forms, and *The Wife's Lament* a possible one out of forty-four.[30] Participles are used mainly as post-modifiers. At the same time although *The Wife's Lament* uses roughly equal numbers of preterite and present verb forms, in both *The Wanderer* and *The Seafarer* over seventy per cent of the finite verb forms are in the present tense.

The reasons for these distribution patterns and their poetic effect vary from poem to poem. So, although narration in the first person, locating the narrative in the speaker's present, is a shared feature, in *The Wanderer* the direct speech itself is placed in a non-specified past by two interventions by the poet. Again all three poems begin with an exposition of the speaker's own past; however, only in *The Wife's Lament* does the subsequent shift to present tense forms relate to the speaker's specific present situation, and only in this poem is there an attempt to follow what may be called narrative order. The woman who says she is now living in an earth-work under an oak-tree traces events step by step from the time of her growing up to her own present situation.[31] In *The Seafarer*, in contrast, there is no development of narrative, the poet's purpose being seemingly 'an imaginative evocation of physical and emotional experiences' to 'illuminate a symbolic passive spiritual truth'.[32] And although the poem is firmly rooted in what may be called the present of performance, in no part of the poem does the speaker's actual 'present' play a significant role.

Thus, in the first part of *The Seafarer* (11.1–33), the dominant tense

---

[30] *Onhweorfan* can be either transitive or intransitive.
[31] I do not agree with Leslie's theory, p. 3, of 'breaks in continuity' here.
[32] See Gordon, p. 10.

is the past—the seafarer-speaker's past, spent travelling in wintry
weather on the sea—contrasted with a hypothetical landsman's
present, comfortable and free from troubles on land (11.12–13 and
27–9). The dominant tense of the second part (11.33b–66a) is the
present, but with the exception of 11.33b–38 and 58–66a (which
frame this section and which relate solely to his state of mind and his
probable future activity—setting out to sea once more) the present is
again not the speaker's present. First we have the universal present,
relating to any point in linear time—there is no one *in the world* who
is not concerned when he undertakes a sea-voyage (11.39–47). Next
we have the present of a hypothetical seafarer, urged by the coming
of summer to set sail, which in its turn is contrasted with the present
of an equally hypothetical and ignorant (lands?)man (11.48–57).
Then in the last part of the poem (11.66 to the end), the speaker's
present is confined to the initial statement of faith:

Ic gelyfe no
þæt him eorðwelan   ece stondað   (11.66–7),

with the verb *stondað* being an example of Old English use of the
present tense with future reference.[33] Subsequently, although the

[33] The seafarer-narrator's attitude towards the landsman and his desire for
a dangerous existence have both to be seen in the context of views such as are
expressed in Ælfric, *CH* I, p. 408 (in a homily drawing its material from
Gregory):

'Verily this following sentence applies to the perishing soul, "On this day
thou dwellest in peace, for the vengeance to come is now hidden from
thine eyes." The perverse soul is indeed dwelling in peace in its day, when
in transient time it rejoices, and is exalted with dignities, and in temporary
enjoyments is immoderate, and is dissolved in fleshly lusts, and is awed by
no fear of future punishment, but hides from itself the miseries following
after; because if it reflect on them, then will worldly bliss be troubled by
that reflection. It has then peace in its day, when it will not afflict the
present mirth with any care for the future unhappiness, but goes with
closed eyes to the penal fire. The soul which in this wise now lives, shall be
afflicted when the righteous rejoice; and all the perishable things which it
now accounts as peace and bliss shall then be turned for it to bitterness and
strife; for it will have great contention with itself, why it would not before
in life with any carefulness foresee the condemnation which it is then
suffering. Concerning which it is written, "Blessed is the man who is ever
fearing; and verily the hardened shall fall into evil." Again in another place
holy writ admonishes, "In all thy works be thou mindful of thy last day,
and in eternity thou wilt not sin."'

dominant tense is the present, it is the present of the typical (aging) mortal and the general conditions in which such a one finds himself, the present of this transitory and progressively weakening world, and the eternal present of God. And when at the end first person forms return once more, they are now in the plural, not 'I' but 'we', involving the poet's audience not just the narrator, with advice as to desirable behaviour if we wish in the future to attain to eternal blessedness. Past forms, except for a single reference to God the creator, are confined to the 'Ubi sunt' passage, and even here present and the resolved perfect tense forms with a finite present tense element predominate. The oppositions of past and present in this poem are thus not those of the narrator's own life.

One of *The Seafarer's* major themes is experience through suffering (appropriately expressed through past tense forms), illustrated in part through its converse, ignorance and general lack of experience (appropriately expressed through timeless 'present', that is, non-past forms). This experience functions as a jumping-off ground and basis for future actions (for which again 'present' tense forms are appropriate, combined here with a few instances of resolved tenses, relating past events to the present and future). In *The Wanderer*, on the other hand, although experience is again a central issue, it is not suffering that is the dominant motif but transience,[34] and this of itself depends on shifting points of time. The three stages in the development of the speaker of the monologue 'through meditation as *anhoga* on his lot, from *modcearig* to *snottor on mode*, who realizes that the only true consolation is to be sought from our Father in Heaven',[35] are set against the backcloth of past, present and future time in this world and the permanence of the world to come. As in *The Seafarer* the individual is set in the context of mankind in general, in the context of a finite world, in the context of infinity. God, the author of linear time, is seen in his role as the initial creator of mankind and the final destroyer of it.[36] The central part of the poem deals with the passing of time, but it ends (and possibly also by inference begins) with references to the permanence of the heavenly kingdom, eternal and

---

[34] See Dunning and Bliss, p. 98. The essential difference between the two poems is illustrated by clause syntax, with *The Seafarer* containing a very high proportion of clauses in which the speaker or another individual is the 'patient', and with *The Wanderer* containing a no less impressively large number of instances where the speaker or another individual is the 'agent'.

[35] See Dunning and Bliss p. 80.

[36] Note in particular 1.85.

outside time. Why then the reliance on a simple opposition of past and non-past with a preponderance of 'present' tense forms and no resolved constructions here?

Part of the answer, I suggest, lies in the poet's approach to his subject. What happened in the past is happening equally in the present and will happen universally in the future. And to convey this truth the poet employs a shifting reference point against which the passing of time from the creation to the end of the world is measured, a 'here and now', a 'present' with its corresponding past and future, but with a stand-point which changes from one part of the poem to another. At the same time, he links past and future with the present through the devices of recollection, dreaming, imaginative anticipation and comparison, exploiting man's capacity to use thought to move out from and beyond his actual position in time and space and to relate events taking place at different points in time and space. He also links past and non-past by shared time-words such as *oft* and *longe*[37] and by the syntactical device of subordination of one clause to another, often through comparison,[38] and he distances the whole from the individual speaker by the framing *cwæþ*.

To begin with the range of points of reference. First of all there is the moment of composition or performance, the present time of the poet/narrator which is normally kept unobtrusive but twice reveals itself to set the bulk of the poem firmly in past time:

> Swa cwæð eardstapa   earfeþa gemyndig,
> wraþra wælsleahta,   winemæga hryre.   (11.6–7)

and

> Swa cwæð snottor on mode;   gesæt him sundor æt rune   (1.111).

Whether or not we accept the beginning and end of the poem as part of the direct speech, everything else is over and done. This is not a direct and personal appeal to the audience by a narrator. Second,

---

[37] See 11.1, 3, 8; 17 and 20; 38 and 40.

[38] Clauses with verbs in the past tense are normally subordinated to main clauses in the present tense, either through syntactical means or (in 11.79–87 and 99) through juxtaposition of two statements, with the subject matter of the second subordinating it to the first. The only exceptions, apart from the two *swa cwæþ* clauses, are 11.8, 36 and 92–3, all possibly corresponding to modern perfects.

there is the moment of articulation of the monologue reported by the poet/narrator, the present time of the wise man. This man uses the present tense in three ways: to refer to his own personal situation, to refer to the more general situation in the world of his own time, and to enunciate universal truths. And just as his monologue is the result of an act of imagination by the poet, so in that monologue the speaker in his turn uses his imagination to create a lordless man, a dreamer and what I will call a thoughtful man, all with their own present reference, and to invent a past for dead warriors in the imagined, typical ruined city of his own present time. Thus, within the monologue we have the speaker's present extended to his own past (11.6–7 and 19f) and distant past (1.22f) and to the general past through present recollection (1.60f); we have the recollections of an imaginary 'typical' person or persons invented by the 'wise man' (11.34f and 90–1); we have an imagined place and its past, with the present set for once in the context of the past (11.73–87). The device of the dream (11.41f. *þinceð him on mode þæt he his mondryhten/ clyppe...*) puts the past directly into the (invented) present, and the subsequent hallucination, when the dreamer waking momentarily supposes he is surrounded by kinsmen, dramatically further blurs the divisions between past and present.

However, the speaker's imagination is not confined to past and present. From 1.64 projection of thought is also from present to future. A man must restrain his behaviour, must not make boasts until he knows clearly where the *thoughts of his heart* will turn. This warning about future behaviour is followed by an imaginative re-creation of the world when it is all waste, made yet again in terms of the present; and the poem ends by moving at last from time to its context, eternity, with a reference to our Father in heaven, in the everlasting timeless present, *þær us eal seo fæstnung stondeð* (1.115).

The poet of *The Wanderer*, therefore, not only recalls the poet, as do the authors of *The Ruin, The Seafarer* and *The Wife's Lament*, he also exploits man's capacity through thought to recreate the past, whether real or imaginary, to picture situations that are present yet distant, to look forward into the future and as a result to acquire understanding and wisdom.[39] He exploits both cyclical and linear time and also the fact that time is all 'present' in eternity. And to do this he takes advantage of the potentialities offered to him by the lexis and the syntax of his age.

[39] Cf. Ambrose's comment, *PL* 14, col. 492, 'Sed etiam futurorum interpres sapientia est, scit praeterita, et de futuris aestimat'.

II

'Love's Labour's Lost': Sweet Understanding and the Five Worthies

RICHARD PROUDFOOT

The spring of 1595 saw the first publication of Sir Philip Sidney's *Defence of Poetry*. Could it be demonstrated that *Love's Labour's Lost* was written after this publication, then the genesis of Shakespeare's sophisticated and 'sourceless' comedy might feasibly be traced to the general spirit, and even to some particular details, of Sidney's treatment of comedy.

Sidney's chosen example of that mingling of delight and laughter which he recommends as the proper aim of comedy is the picture of '*Hercules*, painted with his great beard and furious countenance, in womans attire, spinning at *Omphales* commaundement.'[1] In *Love's Labour's Lost*, Hercules in love serves Armado as a dignifying precedent for his own 'digression' in pursuit of Jacquenetta. The same figure strikes Berowne, in a spirit closer to Sidney's, as an impressively absurd victim of the 'almightie dreadfull little might' (III.i.200) of Cupid.[2] 'Great *Hercules* whipping a Gigge' (IV.iii.165) is an apt image of the King's descent from the posture of warfare against 'the hudge armie of the worldes desires' (I.i.10) to love of the Princess. As incongruous with his youthful academic pretensions are Berowne's next exempla, 'profound *Sallomon*' and '*Nestor*' (IV.iii.166–7). When Hercules at last arrives on stage, in the shrimpish person of Mote, his minority associates him with that other 'signior *Iunio[r]* gyant dwarffe, dan *Cupid*' (III.i.177).

The collocation of arms and arts established in the play's opening speech is further developed in the comic figures of Don Armado and Holofernes, each a fantastical embodiment of one of the young lords' aspirations. Sidney again affords a possible original.

---

[1] G.G. Smith, *Elizabethan Critical Essays* (Oxford, 1904), I.200.

[2] Quotations from Shakespeare are from the facsimile of the 1598 quarto of *Love's Labour's Lost*, ed. W.W. Greg (Oxford, 1957) and from the *Norton Facsimile of the Shakespeare First Folio*, ed. C. Hinman (1968). Line numbers are from the New Arden editions of the plays.

For what is it to make folks gape at a wretched Begger, or a
beggerly Clowne? or, against lawe of hospitality, to iest at straun-
gers, because they speake no English so well as wee doe? what do
we learne? sith it is certaine

> Nil habet infelix paupertas durius in se,
> Quam quod ridiculos homines facit.

But rather a busy louing Courtier, a hartles threatening *Thraso*, a
selfe-wise-seeming schoolemaster, an awry-transformed Trauel-
ler: These if wee sawe walke in stage names, which wee play
naturally, therein were delightfull laughter, and teaching delight-
fulnes.[3]

Later, Shakespeare would still offer the poverty of a Mouldy or the
Frenchman's English of a Dr Caius to the mercies of the understan-
ders, but in *Love's Labour's Lost* he conforms to Sidney's require-
ment. Holofernes is adequately, almost conclusively, defined by
'selfe-wise-seeming schoolemaster'; Boyet, not to speak of the King
and his lords, by 'busy louing Courtier'. '*Thraso*' is part of the
formula for Armado, but as traveller (a facet of the character unex-
plored after I.i) he looks ahead to the melancholy Jaques. The farcical
tone of his entanglement with Jacquenetta and the alarming pace of
the pregnancy which follows their assignation at the lodge confine
their love within the fantastical area of the play. The incongruity of
such a conjunction is more laughably, and more disturbingly, pro-
jected in the dream-dotage of Titania on translated Bottom, while, in
As You Like It, Jaques, so far from figuring as a rival for the affections
of Audrey, becomes concerned spectator, almost chaperone, while
Touchstone, more happily than Costard, is allowed his rout of
William and his nibble at wedlock.
  Whether or not the influence of Sidney can be plausibly alleged,
Love's Labour's Lost shows Shakespeare moving towards an analytic
concern with character greater than we find in his earlier comedies.
In it, he takes a step towards the first comedies of humours, Chapman's *An Humorous Day's Mirth* (1597)—a play pervaded by minor
verbal correspondences with *Love's Labour's Lost*—and Jonson's
Every Man In his Humour (1598). Like *Love's Labour's Lost*, these
comedies, though set respectively in France and Italy (at least in its
1598 version), are concerned with satirical display of English characters and with extending the language of sophisticated comedy to a

---

[3] Smith, *Elizabethan Critical Essays*, I.200–1.

richer and broader portrayal of social life than Lyly, in his court comedies, had even attempted.

Several main themes have been proposed for *Love's Labour's Lost*. 'The social function of language' might do; or 'affectation'; or perhaps 'courtship', as reflecting the aspiration of the leading characters towards cultivated and 'unbarbarous' behaviour and speech, and their pursuit of it in wooing. Whatever the themes, their vehicle is more often debate than action. It takes many forms, from frequent wit-contests to wider contrasts of attitude embodied in the characters or expressed by the action itself.

The characters are less aware than we of 'courtship' as an overriding concern (except the ladies, whose role as spectators approximates to our own and who represent a norm of polite speech and behaviour). For the King of Navarre and his attendant lords, the initial debate is between the contemplative and the active life; for their fantastical hanger-on, Don Armado, it is rather between arms and love. The schoolmaster Holofernes and his parasite Sir Nathaniel, the curate, oppose their self-applauding and shallow ideal of learning to the encroachments of a 'barbarism' which they associate with the unlettered constable, Dull, but which we easily define by contrast with their false ideal as commonsense. At last, self-centred study and vain courtship yield to the stern arguments of death and disease, jest giving way to earnest. The play's themes and its techniques both relate it to its age. Shakespeare's achievement is to give them a richly-imagined human embodiment. His characters are emotionally engaged and consequently debate under the pressure of events, which can—and do—lead some of them to changes of attitude.

William Carroll lists some opposed values which provide debating topics in *Love's Labour's Lost*.[4] They are: learning and experience; affectation and self-knowledge; playing a role and being one's self; style and matter; words and things; rhetoric and simplicity; mind and body; paradox and commonsense; spring and winter. To these might be added: fame and shame; youth and age; arts and arms; the active and the contemplative life. These themes are debated within an action that involves the pursuit of fame, knowledge, and love by a cast which comprises courtiers, ladies, a fantastical soldier, a schoolmaster, a schoolboy, and three uneducated countryfolk. All Shakespeare's stylistic virtuosity is used to define the mixture of wisdom

[4] *The Great Feast of Languages in 'Love's Labour's Lost'* (Princeton, 1976), p. 171.

and folly, truth and affectation, learning and ignorance embodied in each character.

The vestigial action of *Love's Labour's Lost* takes place in the park of a country manor to which the King of Navarre has retired with his three courtiers, Berowne, Demain, and Longaville, in fulfilment of a vow to renounce worldly things (and especially the company of women) for three years, in order to acquire deathless fame by study. To this retreat come the Princess of France and her three ladies, Rosaline, Katherine, and Maria, chaperoned by their usher, Boyet. Her embassy, to negotiate the surrender of Aquitaine by Navarre to her 'decrepit, sicke, and bedred Father' (I.i.137), forces the King to break his vow by meeting her, though he endeavours to salvage the letter of it by lodging her in a tent in the park rather than indoors. At the first interview, the King falls in love with the Princess, as do his three lords with her three ladies (who already know them by reputation and have seen them before with eyes of approval). The outcome seems obvious: the foolish vow of abstinent study will yield to the wisdom of a return to love and to life. This obvious outcome is not to be: 'the catastrophe is' not 'a Nuptiall' (IV.i.76–7). Shakespeare has other ends in view. The King and lords do indeed come to condone their own (and each others') breach of the initial vow, but their success is no greater as lovers than as students. Loading their ladies with poems and love tokens, their reward is to be thoroughly mocked when they come to the Princess's tent, disguised as Russians, to dance and to woo. Their vows of love are misdirected. The ladies too are masked and, by exchange of the lords' tokens, lead them once more into false oaths—which they must once more forswear, having made them to the wrong ladies. The death of the sick king (soon forgotten once the wooing is under way) precipitates an outcome in which 'Iacke hath not Gill' (V.ii.865).

If King and Princess and their retinues are alike far from home, the same is not true of most of the other characters. The exception is the King's eccentric retainer, Don Adriano de Armado, the 'refined trauailer of Spaine' who is to entertain the scholars' leisure hours with 'high borne wordes' of 'the worth of many a Knight:/ From tawnie Spaine lost in the worldes debate' (I.i.162, 171–2). Instead, it is we who are entertained by his ignominious and indecorous surrender to the base charms of Jacquenetta, a dairy-maid. The humiliation of Armado's love is syllogistically justified in soliloquy: 'as it is base for a Souldier to loue; so am I in loue with a base wench' (I.ii.54–6).

Jacquenetta has another suitor, '*Costard* the swaine', also a servant of the King, engaged, like Armado, for the honest recreation of the scholar-courtiers. No sooner have the King and his lords signed their 'compact' of renunciation than their oath is doubly challenged, first by news of the impending arrival of the Princess, then by the entry of the parish constable, Antony Dull, with Costard (under arrest) and a letter from Armado. He has taken Costard '*sorted and consorted contrary to thy established proclaymed Edict and continent Cannon . . . With a childe of our Grandmother Eue, a female; or for thy more sweete vnderstanding a Woman*' (I.i.249–54)—or, as Costard puts it, more succinctly, 'a Wench'. Until Act V, the lords and ladies encounter Armado only through his letters. When he appears, it is in the company of a schoolboy page, Mote, whose repartee reveals his master's alienation from mundane reality.[5]

Mote (whose name means 'mote', or speck of flying dust; 'moth'; and French *mot*, 'word') and Costard ('apple'; hence 'head', in slang usage, and thus 'mother wit' or 'commonsense') are Shakespeare's commentators on the absurdity of Armado. Costard is further used as a foil for both court parties. He appears in the latter part of every scene in the play but II.i, generally to bathetic effect. The full absurdity of Armado's love for Jacquenetta lies in the contrast between his flourishes of rhetoric and her inability to utter anything but the tritest of clichés.[6] Bar Dull, who has in the proverbial Elizabethan phrase 'wit enough to be a constable', Jacquenetta is the least articulate character in this comedy of words. In their own way, though, both reveal a greater grasp on reality than their verbal superiors Armado and Holofernes.

The other local characters are a forester, the schoolmaster, Holofernes, and the curate, Sir Nathaniel. Holofernes is a full anglicization of the Italian comic 'pedant', as is Sir Nathaniel of the flattering parasite of Latin New Comedy. We first meet the two 'men of learning' in the revealing company of Dull. The success of the Princess in shooting a deer launches Holofernes into poetical improvisation, while Nathaniel fends off Dull, whose inarticulacy provides the empty words of the pedant with an ambiguous resonator. The 'gyft' or 'talent' claimed by the extemporal poet himself and his admirer, the curate, is seen as a matter of mere

[5] For modernization to Mote, see *Love's Labour's Lost*, ed. J. Kerrigan (Harmondsworth, 1982), note on I.ii stage direction, pp. 160–1.

[6] See F.P. Wilson, *Shakespearian and Other Studies*, ed. H. Gardner (Oxford, 1969), 68, 115.

elaboration of verbal patterns. Direct relation to the subject survives in the first six lines of Holofernes' 'extemporall Epytaph on the death of the Deare' (IV.ii.57–62), but after that the only concern is with prosodic and mathematical ingenuity. Nowhere does Shakespeare reveal more clearly than in the idiom of the minor figures of *Love's Labour's Lost* his endorsement of the attitude reflected in Ben Jonson's memorable phrase, '*Language* most shewes a man: speake that I may see thee'.[7]

More obviously than their counterparts in *A Midsummer Night's Dream*, the tradesmen of Athens, the 'irregular humorists' of *Love's Labour's Lost* exist outside, or at best in parallel with, its main plot. A summary of the action could, without damage, omit all mention of them until the final scene, when they present the show of the Nine Worthies—or, more exactly, the Five Worthies. The innumeracy of Costard gives Shakespeare a simple way of establishing Berowne's mocking superiority to the Worthies, but the reason why the Nine Worthies are no more than Five remains a pretty reason. It is, of course, that there are only five performers (discounting the discreet contribution of Dull's drum) and that a main point of the show is to display them in turn in their varying attempts to match the worth of their roles, or at least to run the gauntlet of their 'gentle' audience.

Shakespeare uses these characters much as he had used the servants, Launce and Speed, in *The Two Gentlemen of Verona*. They perform minor functions in the action, such as carrying letters, and they afford, by implicit parallel and explicit comment, a foil for the events and characters of the main action. But they have a third and more pervasive use: to embody important areas of the plays' metaphoric language. The servants in *Two Gentlemen* (and the dog) provide prosaic physical points of reference for the language of love-service used by their callow masters. *Love's Labour's Lost* offers a wider variety of such effects. Thus Armado is soldier, traveller, poet and 'Fashions owne knight' (I.i.177), who has no shirt beneath the outward flamboyance of the 'plume of fethers' (IV.i.93). His is the most pervasive presence in the play's language, but domineering pedant, night-watch constable and boy are also recurring images in the language of love. Sir Nathaniel and Jacquenetta stand slightly outside this pattern. His role is determined by dependence on Holofernes, which leads to an emphasis on his little learning and its dangers rather than on his religious office.

[7] *Discoveries*, in *Ben Jonson*, ed. C.H. Herford, P. & E. Simpson, 11 vols (Oxford, 1925–52), VIII, 625.

Jacquenetta contributes less to the imagery, but she has greater thematic importance. She adumbrates the significance of other, later heroines of Shakespearian comedy, Mariana in *Measure for Measure* or Helena in *All's Well that Ends Well* (still a dark horse among contenders for identification as the lost *Love's Labour's Won*). These determined lovers' loss of virginity, by cutting one knot, makes another eternal. By leading Angelo and Bertram blindfold into supposed fornication, they break down the obstacle that separates them from long-desired husbands and their plays from a catastrophe of even qualified happiness. Jacquenetta enters *her* play already, and to all appearance happily, no virgin, and leaves it as the only girl to get her man.

In *All's Well*, Bertram, wishing to escape from enforced marriage to Helena, imposes on her conditions whose fulfilment will alone lead him to acknowledge her as his wife.

> *When thou canst get the Ring vpon my finger, which neuer shall come off, and shew mee a childe begotten of thy bodie, that I am father too, then call me husband:* (III.ii.56–8)

His conditions might be paraphrased as 'when you can prove yourself my wife *de facto*, then I shall acknowledge you'. The impossible tasks themselves define the condition of marriage and present Helena rather with a challenge than a final rejection. The very language of Bertram's letter to his mother hints at a similar underlying ambivalence: '*I haue wedded her, not bedded her, and sworne to make the not eternall*' (II.ii.20–1). Bertram's lust for Diana gives Helena her opportunity to win ring and child and to convert eternal '*not*' to 'knot'. The auditory pun can disappear in silent reading, but Shakespeare seems to imply Bertram's unconscious readiness to accept Helena. Helena rises successfully to the challenge, to be accepted, at last, as wife in fact as well as in name—'Both, both, O pardon' (V.iii.302).

In *Love's Labour's Lost*, Armado is revealed by a similar unconscious pun. Describing Jacquenetta to the King in his first letter, he states one of the play's major themes with his words '*or for thy more sweet vnderstanding a Woman*' (I.i.253–4). 'Understanding' was a hackneyed joke in relation to the unlettered 'understanding gentlemen' who stood to watch the play from the yard that surrounded the stage. Equally available was the overtly sexual sense which commentators are still blind to in this passage (despite the clue of '*as my euer esteemed duetie prickes me on*' (254–5)). The 'sweet understanding' of a 'conjunction copulative', with its issue in carnal 'knowledge' (and pregnancy), is thus, from the outset, directly contrasted with the unseasonable and sterile vow to study in segregated celibacy. Costard and Jacquenetta have such understanding already. Armado will have it too, by the time the play is done and the Spaniard's rapier, after an aberrant lapse into prose-poet's pen, has found its fruitful decorum as ploughshare.

Acts III and IV hinge on verbal composition. The King and lords write love-poems to their ladies; Berowne even sends his to Rosaline. He picks the unlettered Costard as his postman, ignorant that Armado too has charged him with a love-letter to the equally illiterate Jacquenetta. Naturally, the letters are misdelivered, Rosaline receiving Armado's lecture on love the leveller of kings and beggars, Jacquenetta, Berowne's sonnet. Both are publicly read and both are ridiculed, Armado's letter by the ladies and Boyet, Berowne's poem, more equivocally, by the rival poet, Holofernes. These amusements lead to the first major climax of the play, in IV.iii.

The play's bitter-sweet tone in its handling of love owes much to the development of Berowne, in the middle acts, as alternately scourge and evangelist of love. Shakespeare here uses a favourite technique, the thrusting of a character into prominence and emotional complexity by means of a pair of soliloquies, separated by an unconnected scene or two. Discounting Richard of Gloucester, whose two soliloquies in *3 Henry VI* provide the climaxes of the play's two halves, the first notable example is in *The Two Gentlemen of Verona*, where two soliloquies serve to introduce the double infidelity of Proteus to Julia and to Valentine. Proteus moves from enthusiasm about his love for Silvia (II.iv.188–210) to fuller awareness of its more serious consequences (II.vi). Similarly, the bravura of Berowne's verse soliloquy (III.i.170–202) yields to a deeper sense of his shame and folly in the prose speech which opens IV.iii. A much later, and more penetrating, use of the technique is in the two speeches which plumb the hidden depths of Angelo and lead him from the inception of desire for Isabella to preparedness for lust in action (*Measure for Measure*, II.ii.162–87; II.iv.1–29). All three characters are oath-breakers. But where the perilous treachery of Proteus and Angelo can seem, in retrospect, a fortunate fall, Berowne's more natural failing leads to no fifth-act betrothal or marriage.

Alone of the lords, Berowne is shown facing up to the dilemma presented by love. He does so, with a characteristic mingling of

scepticism and acceptance, in the first soliloquy, after his dispatch of
the sonnet to Rosaline.

> O and I forsooth in loue, I that haue been loues whip?
> A verie Bedell to a humerous sigh, a Crietick, nay a night-watch
>   Constable,
> A domineering pedant ore the Boy, then whom no mortall so
>   magnificent.   (III.i.170–5)

What follows is more personal, but these opening lines must strike us
by their comprehensive association of his lost role as love's rebel
with pedant and constable, while he identifies his enemy, Cupid,
with boy and magnifico. Nowhere else in the play does Shakespeare
give so clear a clue to the thematic coherence of his sub-plot.
Berowne's conclusion reflects a degree of acceptance.

> Well, I will loue, write, sigh, pray, shue, grone,
> Some men must loue my Ladie, and some Ione.   (201–2)

Berowne is thus set up as the proper supervisor of the play's first
change of direction, observing as each of his three companions in
turn reveals (in supposed solitude) his love for one of the ladies and
his skill as a love poet. By the time the fourth lover, Dumain, reads
his poem, all three others are watching. The joke accumulates as, one
by one, Longaville, the King, and Berowne 'step foorth to whip
hipocrisie' (IV.iii.149). We, of course, can foresee the bursting of the
bubble of Berowne's self-righteousness even before the arrival of
Costard and Jacquenetta to deliver his treasonable sonnet to the King
on the orders of Holofernes. Each lover in turn seeks justification for
breaking his oath. Longaville, like Chaucer's Arcite, argues that
Maria's divinity frees him:

> A Woman I forswore, but I will proue,
> Thou being a Goddesse, I forswore not thee. (IV.iii.62–3)

Dumain finds in Katherine a perfection which would lead Jove to
renounce his godhead. Berowne develops the defence of perjury by
amplifying the theme that the original oath was 'Flat treason gainst
the kingly state of youth' and that 'It is Religion to be thus for-
sworne' (IV.iii.290, 360).

One phase of folly may now have ended in the lords' belated
concession that 'euery man with his affectes is borne/ Not by might

mastred, but by speciall grace' (I.i.150–1), but their love poems have revealed an affectation in wooing equal to that of the vow to study. Berowne may argue in favour of living reality, but his argument is still a piece of sophistry, so framed as to undermine the seriousness and good sense of the position he is urging. When the men determine to 'woe these gyrles of Fraunce' (IV.iii.368), the military images and their enthusiasm in adoption of new roles must recall the conviction with which two of them earlier accepted the King's challenge to 'warre against your owne affections,/ And the hudge armie of the worldes desires' (I.i.9–10) (not to mention the martial precedent of Armado's subjection to Jacquenetta). Berowne, as usual, sees farthest ahead. As they leave to devise 'Reuels, Daunces, Maskes, and merrie houres', his parting words are 'Light Wenches may proue plagues to men fors[w]orne,/ If so our Copper byes no better treasure' (IV.iv.376, 382–3). Even he doesn't see that the 'copper' of broken oaths will not be alone in inviting the ladies' mockery. As wooers too, they are about to be proved fools.

The revels projected by the King and lords are soon supplemented by a further 'eruption, and sodaine breaking out of myrth' in what it pleases Armado to designate 'the *posteriors* of this day' (V.i.109–10, 84). As he seeks the aid of Holofernes in devising 'some delightful ostentation, or show, or pageant, or antique, or fierworke' (106–8), all the play's subsidiary characters (except Jacquenetta) are brought together on stage for the first time. The meeting of Armado and Holofernes initiates a verbal orgy. As Mote puts it, 'They haue been at a great feast of Languages, and stolne the scraps' (37–8). Though deaf to their own excesses, they have keen ears for them in each other. To Holofernes, the Spaniard seems 'vaine, ridiculous, & thrasonicall' (13) in general and, in particular, given to drawing 'out the thred of his verbositie, finer then the staple of his argument' (17–18). Conversely, Armado complains that 'the Schoolemaister is exceeding fantasticall, Too too vaine, too too vaine:' (V.ii.524–5). So, while the lords prepare to incur the ladies' mockery in their Russian disguises, 'The Pedant, the Bragart, the Hedge-Priest, the Foole, and the Boy' (536–7) are found fit by Holofernes to impersonate the Nine Worthies. Modestly, he volunteers to make good the deficiency in numbers by playing three himself ('Thrice worthie Gentleman' (V.i.138)). The Nine Worthies—nine famous heroes of antiquity, three biblical, three classical and three from the world of medieval romance—had become, by 1595, something of a cliché, if not merely a joke. No doubt Shakespeare's choice of this *topos* for his fantastics' show reflected the real risks run by an English sovereign on progress confronted with the zeal of amateur village actors. But in *Love's Labour's Lost* the theme of 'worth' is pervasive: and it is often linked with the search for classical or biblical precedents for action. Armado seeks comfort in the reflection that if love is too much for him, 'yet was *Sampson* so tempted, and he had an excellent strength: Yet was *Salomon* so seduced, and he had a very good wit. *Cupids* Butshaft is too hard for *Hercules* Clubb, and therefore too much oddes for a Spaniards Rapier' (I.ii.163–6). Berowne too hits on Hercules, 'whipping a Gigge' (IV.iii.165) or 'Still clyming trees in the *Hesperides*' (338) in subservience to love. This may help to account for the uncanonical presence of Hercules among Holofernes' Worthies (as the pun on 'pumpkin' and the comically fruitful confusion of 'great' and 'big' explain the presence of the other outsider, Pompey, played by the great-limbed clown, Costard).

The final scene of *Love's Labour's Lost* is the longest in all Shakespeare. It consists of a series of interrupted actions, culminating in the ladies' withholding of love. First, the ladies wonder at the folly of their lovers, then Boyet announces their approach, in disguise. He remains as an amused spectator of the discomfiture of the 'Muscovites', playing his own part in disconcerting Mote into losing his lines. Rosaline, in the guise of the Princess, mocks the King and teases the men with her refusal to dance. The lords retire in confusion, each having sworn his love to the wrong lady. Now costumes are changed: the ladies resume their true identities and the lords return 'in their own shapes' (V.iii.288), dressed no longer as scholars, nor Russians but—for the first time in the play, perhaps—as the courtiers they are. Seeking to avoid more mockery, the men confess that they were indeed the Russians, only to be shamed with the charge of a second perjury. Once more, Berowne tries to save the day by changing the terms of the conflict.

> Thus pooure the Starres downe plagues for periurie.
> Can anie face of brasse hold longer out?
> . . .
> O neuer will I trust to speaches pend,
> Nor to the motion of a Schoole-boyes tongue:
> Nor neuer come in vizard to my friend,
> Nor woo in rime like a blind harpers songue.
> Taffata phrases, silken tearmes precise,
> Three pilde Hi[p]erboles, spruce affection:
> Figures pedanticall, these sommer flies,

Haue blowne me full of maggot ostentation.
I do forsweare them, and I here protest,
By this white Gloue (how white the hand God knowes)
Hencefoorth my wooing minde shalbe exprest
In russet yeas, and honest kersie noes.
And to begin Wench, so God helpe me law,
My loue to thee is sound, *sance* cracke or flaw.
    Rosa. *Sans, sans,* I pray you.
    Bero. Yet I haue a tricke,
Of the olde rage; beare with me, I am sicke.
Ile leaue it by degrees;   (394–5, 402–18)

This speech tries, as the metaphors of clothing indicate, to replace the poetical affectations of the lords' previous attempts at courtship with an equally inappropriate (and inconsistent) affectation of plain-speaking. At this pass, the arrival of the Worthies offers a valuable diversion and lords and ladies sit, together at last, to form the on-stage audience for 'one show worse then the Kings and his company' (509).

Shakespeare now has all his characters in play. The effect of the pageant is complex. On one level, it submits each of its performers to the judgement of the on-stage audience. Costard and Moth come off relatively unscathed, while the more pretentious Nathaniel and Holofernes are shamed by the inventive heckling of the lords, now reconciled with Boyet in mockery of the lower orders. But as the lords mock on and the shades of evening begin to invade the dialogue, the image of the famous dead, however inadequately pro-jected, makes its own comment on the King's futile ambition for a fame to 'all eternitie' (I.i.7). The first surprise comes when Holofernes, soundly mocked out of the 'Maccabeus' to qualify his 'Judas', turns on his deriders with 'This is not generous, not gentle, not humble' (621). He may stumble at his exit, and humility has never been his own strong suit, but his parting shot is on target. From the fooleries of self-regarding scholarship (of which Holofernes has more than his fair share) and those of poetical court-ship (where their cautionary magnifying mirror is rather Armado), the lords have now sunk from the courtesy proper to their station to the vulgar mocking vanity of a mere gentleman-usher, one who 'peckes vp Wit as Pidgions Pease' (315).

From Armado, as Hector of Troy, their jibes provoke an even less expected and more impressive rebuke. The fantastic braggart rises to a truly human estimate of the worth of dead Hector: 'The sweete

War-man is dead and rotten, Sweete chucks beat not the bones of the
buried: When he breathed he was a man' (651–3). Now that his five
actors have appeared, Shakespeare has no need to prolong the
pageant, but his way of curtailing it comes as a total surprise. Costard
runs in to announce that Jacquenetta is two months pregnant and to
challenge Armado to fight him: 'the childe bragges in her bellie
already: tis yours' (666–7). It is Armado's turn to be shamed in
public, not only for improbably getting Jacquenetta with child but
for his reluctance to fight in his shirt: 'The naked trueth of it is, I
ha[u]e no Shirt' (699). This revelation, which matches Berowne's
renunciation of 'Taffata phrases', is the play's last blow against
stylistic affectation, its last opening of the hollowness of a verbal
pretension which merely attempts to conceal absence of meaning.

As the quarrel between Costard and Armado reaches its farcical
climax, a black-clad figure has been moving slowly, unobserved,
onto the stage and towards the Princess. As the laughter at Armado's
confusion dies down, he speaks.

> *Marcad.* God saue you Madame.
> *Quee.* Welcome *Marcade*, but that thou
> interr[u]pptest our merriment.
> *Marcad.* I am sorie Madame for the newes I bring
> is heauie on my tongue. The King your father
> *Quee.* Dead for my life.
> *Marcad.* Euen so: my tale is tolde.
> *Ber.* Worthies away, the Scaene begins to cloude.
>
> (705–12)

This is Shakespeare's last trick. It is nearly his last move, too, in the
debate between book-learning and experience. All now changes.
With the 'quickness' of Jacquenetta and the death of the King of
France, reality, as well as night, creeps in upon the 'lytlle Achademe'
(I.i.13). The naming of the messenger seems hardly warranted for a
character with so brief a role. Critics have accordingly sought for
meaning in the name itself. One possibility might be 'Mar
Arcady'—if the play gave, as it does not, any sense of the Arcadian
(though Death's threat '*et in Arcadia ego*' may be seen as relevant).
Altogether likelier is an allusion to the god Mercury, messenger of
the gods and leader of the souls of the dead to the underworld.
Certainly garbling of the name Mercury to 'Markedy' is found in a
court play of the early 1590s, Robert Wilson's *The Cobbler's Prophecy*
(printed in 1594), whose main theme, the rivalry between arts and

arms, also bears on the broader concerns of *Love's Labour's Lost*.[8]

After Marcade has delivered his news, the play enters its final phase. The arrival of death might seem an indecorously sombre note to end so high-spirited and artificial a comedy. But the play began with the aspiration of the King and his lords to conquer death and time.

> Let Fame, that all hunt after in their lyues,
> Liue registred vpon our brazen Tombes,
> And then grace vs, in the disgrace of death:
> When spight of cormorant deuouring Time,
> Thendeuour of this present breath may buy:
> That honour which shall bate his sythes keene edge,
> And make vs heires of all eternitie.   (I.i.1–7)

Now time runs out, as the Princess finds 'the latest minute of the houre' 'A time ... too short,/ To make a world-without-end bargaine in' (V.ii.777–80). The King's last pleas for love lead the Princess to reveal that she has taken the men's wooing as mere 'courtship pleasant iest and courtecie,/ As bombast and as lyning to the time' (770–1). Then she relents, to the point of offering her lover hope, but on strict conditions. And so the action ends with the men bound to a year and a day's penance and hardship, the King in a hermitage, Berowne in a hospital, jesting to 'the pained impotent' and 'the speachlesse sicke' (844, 841). Shame, and the witty renunciation of affectation, are insufficient penance for vanity and for the lords' over-estimate of their own worth. More exactly, abuse of speech is to be purged by its use in the interests of those that lack it.

Denial of the conventional happy ending of comedy may offend Berowne—'these Ladies courtesie/ Might well haue made our sport a Comedie' (865–6)—but it is no arbitrary *tour-de-force* on Shakespeare's part. His action (and their language) has consistently revealed the young men's immaturity, side-by-side with the ladies' awareness that they may prove capable of growing up. A year of self-effacement in preparation for marriage, and of submission to those hard aspects of reality so carefully excluded from their 'lytlle Achademe', age, sickness and death, is decorum.

Before lords and ladies can part, Armado returns, having 'vowde

---

[8] J.M. Nosworthy, 'The Importance of Being Marcade', *Shakespeare Survey* 32 (1979), 105–14; A. Barton, 'A Source for *Love's Labour's Lost*', *TLS*, 24 November 1978, 1373–4.

to *Iacquenetta* To holde the Plough for her sweete loue three yeere' (873–4). Of the men in *Love's Labour's Lost*, he alone achieves his comic happy ending and moves from the enclosed world of the King's park not to the grimmer enfolding of hermitage or hospital, but to the farmland of the surrounding countryside. If the Folio's added last line for him, 'You that way; we this way', is authentic, it can be used by the play's one successful lover to separate himself from its failures. The theme of disparity in love is resolved here in terms which discourage too close analysis. Jacquenetta remains inscrutable. She is last seen and heard, in IV.iii, in the familiar company of Costard (unless her presence is required, as it is certainly invited, by the '*Enter all*' which cues the final songs). Again, we are carried forward to those later and more deeply troubled comedies, *Measure for Measure* and *All's Well that Ends Well*: both to the louder silences of Isabella and Bertram and to love's levelling of ranks in a bed where 'both not sinne, and yet a sinfull fact' (*All's Well*, III.vii.47). Angelo's ancestry, too, strangely combines the oath-breaking infidelity of Berowne (or Proteus) with the deceptive out-side of Armado. His outside is more plausible than Armado's, his pursuit of love more sinister, but in the end the exposure of his 'gravity' makes him weigh level with the unjustly repudiated Mariana, against whom he has imputed 'levity'. Armado emerges the stronger of the two, to preside over his play's last scene. Angelo has to submit to the superior power of the Duke and to his urgings to love the wife whose worth is 'worth yours' (*Measure for Measure*, V.i.495).

The broken ends of wooing and pageant are alike healed by the play's conclusion, the dialogue compiled by 'the two Learned men ... in prayse of the Owle and the Cuckow' (V.ii.876–7). No contem-porary setting of these songs survives, if indeed they were meant to be sung. They constitute a kind of epilogue—and a richly satisfying one. In them, for the first time, we see the life of the countryside outside the walls of the King's park and hear the unaffected notes of the birds. The dialogue strikes a quizzical balance between Spring and Winter, reversing expectation yet again, so that spring is cel-ebrated by the mocking song of the cuckoo and winter by the 'merrie note' of the owl, emblem alike of wisdom and folly. The play's last debate moves from the game of wit to the natural opposition of the seasons, bringing this long scene to a close with the first of its component units not to be interrupted before its end.

III

'So Careful of the Type?'—Victorian Biblical Typology: Sources and Applications

G.B. TENNYSON

The OED entries for the words *typology* and *typological*, give as the earliest date for the use of each the year 1845. In both cases the work cited in illustration of that first use is Patrick Fairbairn's *The Typology of Scripture*, which first appeared in that year.[1] The OED defines the word *typology* as: 'The study of symbolic representation, *esp.* of the origin and meaning of scripture; also *transf.*, symbolic significance, or treatment, symbolism.' For *typological* the OED offers: 'Of or pertaining to typology; relating to the study or interpretation of symbols.' The important citation from Fairbairn is the one on *typology*, which is in fact the opening sentence of Fairbairn's book. It reads: 'The typology of Scripture has been one of the most neglected departments of theological science.' Thus, 'typology' and 'typological' both make their first official appearance in the language in the mid-nineteenth century; and yet, despite the fact that these two words appear to be 'Victorian' words, it is nevertheless true that until recently one could say, adapting Fairbairn, that the study of Victorian typology has been one of the most neglected departments of literary science.

But neglect no longer describes the scholarly situation, for in the past several years there has been a great stirring of interest in the study of typology in Victorian literature and art. Books and articles have come forth in something approaching abundance; and Victorian typology has been the subject of sessions at meetings of professional scholarly societies. More than a century and a quarter after Fairbairn coined the word, the matter of typology in Fairbairn's own age has come into its own.

But, of course, Fairbairn almost certainly did not coin the word, and he positively did not invent the practice. What we today refer to as typology, or more specifically biblical typology—the practice of seeing Old Testament persons and events as foreshadowing persons

---

[1] Fairbairn's book went through many editions in the nineteenth century and was reprinted again in 1976.

and events in the New Testament—is as old as Christianity itself. That the word *typology* does not appear to have been used in earlier times is but a reflection of how much the practice we designate by the word was previously simply a part of the furniture of the mind. It was not necessary to coin the word until the practice it denotes was no longer something to be taken for granted, rather as Browning said of words of this sort—those ending in '-ogony' and '-ology'—they sport 'Greek endings, each the little passing-bell/ That signifies some faith's about to die.' The faith that was about to die in the case of typology had been alive indeed for eighteen centuries and was flourishing more than Fairbairn realized in his own day. The lexical evidence for the antiquity of typology absent under the entry for the word itself will be found under the primary words *type, figure*, and *shadow*, which bear fourteenth- and fifteenth-century citations from authors like Chaucer, Wycliffe, and Robert Henryson. All that Fairbairn can be said to have introduced is the study of the practice, not the practice itself. One could say that prior to the nineteenth century one did not study typology, one perceived types.

From the nineteenth-century addition of the passing-bell of '-ology' to the idea of types, scholarship has recapitulated in little more than a century the long history of typology itself. Just as typology began as a purely scriptural matter but found expression in ecclesiastical art and eventually in secular literature, so the study of typology moved from biblical hermeneutics to art history and, in our own century, to literary history, chiefly that of the Middle Ages and the Renaissance. Today typology and its near relations, symbol and allegory, are firmly established aspects of the study of earlier literature, albeit still debated aspects in terms of extent and particulars of application.[2] Until recently, however, it was argued that typology, along with allegory, had largely died out after the Reformation and had ceased to be an operative factor in any of the areas

[2] The list of works touching on mediaeval and Renaissance typology is too lengthy to present here, but interested readers may consult the special number of *Studies in the Literary Imagination*, Vol. 3, No. 1 (1975), devoted to 'Typology and Medieval Literature', for a view of the current state of the subject. For post-mediaeval treatments, see Barbara Kiefer Lewalski, *Protestant Poetics and the Seventeenth-Century Religious Lyric* (Princeton, 1979), and for works on early American literary uses of typology, see the bibliography in Sacvan Bercovitch's *Typology and Early American Literature* (Amherst, Ma., 1972). For a comprehensive discussion of the character of biblical typology, see Northrop Frye, *The Great Code: The Bible and Literature* (New York, 1982), esp. Chs. 4 and 5, pp. 78–138.

where it had hitherto reigned supreme, from biblical hermeneutics, to religious art, to secular literature. For a time this deterred scholars from considering the subject in art and literature after the seventeenth century. Lately, however, numerous scholars have argued, and argued persuasively, that typology did not really die out after the Reformation, although it did undergo a kind of sea change, becoming in some sense Protestantized. These scholars have found typological elements flourishing in American colonial literature, in eighteenth-century hymnody, and especially in Victorian visual arts and literature. There is even an essay on typology in twentieth-century literature.[3]

My concern here is precisely with the question of the origins and applications of typology in the Victorian age. Scholars, familiar with the work done to date on Victorian typology—most notably that of George Landow[4]—know that the general line of argument on the Victorian revival of typology runs as follows: Victorian typology is a consequence of the Evangelical movement in the eighteenth and nineteenth centuries. Through hymns and sermons Evangelicals spread typological readings of scripture into virtually every factory and hamlet, and especially into the house in Herne Hill occupied by the Ruskin family. The Evangelicals adhered to what can be called the strict constructionist approach to typology that Protestantism had advocated from the time of the Reformation, that is, typology was *not* allegorical, it did *not* involve the four-fold method of reading scripture; it preferred one-to-one types and antitypes, especially those types from the Old Testament that foreshadowed Christ. Up to now, investigations of Victorian typology have flourished mainly in regard to the visual art of the Pre-Raphaelites and the writings of Ruskin, and more recently Carlyle. The latter's *Past and Present*, for example, has lately been treated as an elaborate typological reading

---

[3] See Earl Miner, ed. *Literary Uses of Typology* (Princeton, 1977). This volume contains essays on typology from the Middle Ages to the twentieth century.

[4] Of Landow's works on this topic, see especially his *William Holman Hunt and Typological Symbolism* (New Haven, 1979). Pp. 186–7 contain a bibliography of works on 'Typology, Allegory and Victorian Religion.' See also Landow's *Victorian Types, Victorian Shadows* (Boston and London, 1980) in which he enlarges the conception of typology and allows for a greater role on the part of Tractarians and High Churchmen, though even here he credits Evangelicalism (p. 20). See also Landow's *Images of Crisis: Literary Iconology, 1750 to the Present* (Boston and London, 1982).

of British history, whereby the twelfth century is the type, so to speak, and the nineteenth is the antitype.[5]

The foregoing is an abbreviated but, I think, not unfair summary of the general position being advanced about Victorian typology. Commentators on the matter not only uniformly assert the Evangelical origins of typology, some even go so far as to pinpoint all Pre-Raphaelite, and by implication most later Victorian, typology at that moment in 1846 when William Holman Hunt read the passage in the second volume of the work by an 'Oxford undergraduate' called *Modern Painters* in which Ruskin explains 'typologically' Tintoretto's *The Annunciation*.

I do not seek to dispute the obvious signs of typological, figural, and symbolic scriptural elements in Victorian art and literature so much as to raise some questions and suggest some considerations that broaden the subject by taking it out of its present narrow home in Evangelical sectarianism. To that end, I offer, first, some objections to the received view of Victorian typology, and then some considerations bearing on its wider dispersal in the age.

On the matter of the encounter between Holman Hunt and *Modern Painters*: it is highly unlikely in principle that anything so widespread as typological and symbolic elements in Pre-Raphaelite art alone, to say nothing of the many other areas in which commentators have found such elements, could stem from a single event in the life of William Holman Hunt. Even the current students of Victorian typology have allowed that Hunt to some extent merely found expressed in Ruskin what he had been exposed to in various ways in his own religious background. But more problematic than that is the Ruskin passage from *Modern Painters* itself. It is not in any strict sense typological. It is allegorical. Here is the key passage:

> ... the whole symmetry of [the painting depends] on a narrow line of light, the edge of a carpenter's square, which connects these unused tools with an object at the top of the brickwork, a white stone, four square, the corner-stone of the old edifice, the base of

[5] In Herbert Sussman, *Fact into Figure: Typology in Carlyle, Ruskin, and the Pre-Raphaelite Brotherhood* (Columbus, Ohio, 1979). The difficulties inherent in such a typological reading are evident from the start. Apart from the non-biblical character of the subject matter, the real obstacle lies in the simple fact that Carlyle hardly sought to present the nineteenth century as any kind of fulfilment of the promise of the twelfth. 'Typological,' then, is being expanded to mean 'sequential and somehow related in time.'

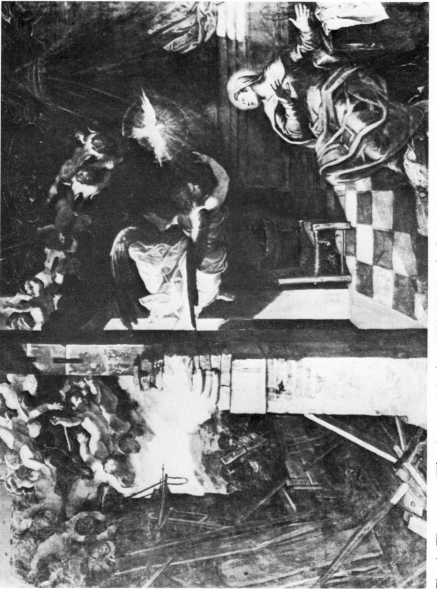

Fig. 1. Tintoretto: 'The Annunciation', c. 1582–87 (*Scuola di San Rocco, Venice*)

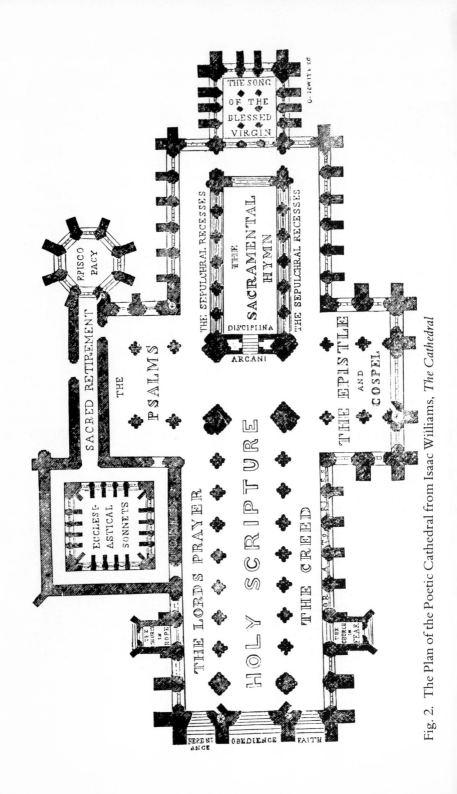

Fig. 2. The Plan of the Poetic Cathedral from Isaac Williams, *The Cathedral*

its supporting column. This, I think, sufficiently explains the typical character of the whole. The ruined house is the Jewish dispensation; that obscurely arising in the dawning of the sky is the Christian; but the corner-stone of the old building remains, though the builder's tools lie idle beside it, and the stone which the builders refused is become the Headstone of the Corner.[6] [Fig. 1]

Ruskin, then, is explaining the Tintoretto painting in terms of what the objects in it *stand for* at least as much as he is explaining it in terms of what the objects *prefigure* or *shadow forth*. Insofar as the painting does self-evidently shadow forth something, it shadows forth an event in the New Testament in terms of a prior event in the same New Testament. To say (as Ruskin, by the way, does *not* say) that the Annunciation prefigures the Nativity is but to say that conception precedes birth. Quite; but this is not either Protestant or Catholic typology. Nor is there in the painting a single figure—neither the Virgin nor the Angel—that is a received Old Testament type of Christ, which is the kind of typological reading most congenial to Evangelicals. What we have at best in the Ruskin discussion is evidence of a typological and figural disposition, that is, a tendency to seek signs, symbols, and allegories in religious art. Ruskin gives his interpretation a typological *flavour*, to be sure, by adapting Psalm 118:22, which reads: 'The stone which the builders refused is become the head stone of the corner', so that a passage in the Old Testament can be seen as anticipating the New. Moreover, judging from the apparently rabbinical figures in the centre-left of the picture, Tintoretto may well have had just such a correspondence in mind. But this kind of correspondence has at least as much in common with traditional pre-Reformation allegorical and symbolic interpretations as it has with Evangelicalism; for what is being typologically anticipated is the founding of a new *church*, not the anticipation of one historical person by another, the alleged speciality of evangelical typological reading. Of course, Tintoretto himself has more in common with pre-Reformation attitudes than with evangelical ones, albeit that he was, needless to add, a *post*-Raphaelite.

Thus, the localizing of Victorian typology in the Ruskin–Hunt axis proves on examination to be a slender reed on which to hang so much. And even if it is taken as merely itself a symbol for the

[6] John Ruskin, *Works*, ed. E.T. Cook and Alexander Wedderburn, 39 vols. (London, 1903–12), 4: 264–5.

Evangelical source for Victorian typology, that source itself needs reassessment. Modern scholars have used it rather too freely. Whenever they find typological elements in other Victorians that cannot be traced to Holman Hunt and the Pre-Raphaelites, they simply unearth an Evangelical parent or point to a vague, general Evangelical influence. Having done so, they go on to give readings and interpretations that are scarcely Evangelical at all, though, as we have seen, in this they have been preceded, if not prefigured, by Ruskin himself.

One way out of the dual dilemma of Evangelical sources for all typological readings coupled with readings that are not Evangelical or even strictly typological is to seek other grounds for the Victorian use of typological and scriptural materials in art and life. These grounds are readily available, though largely ignored, in the theory and practice of the Oxford Movement. It is the analogical and typological outlook of that movement to which I should like to draw attention as at least a parallel source for the Victorian exaltation of the ancient mode of typology and its relatives.

Several commentators have recently pointed to the aesthetic and literary dimensions of the Oxford Movement as having exercised great influence in the Victorian age. I have myself placed particular emphasis on two central Tractarian doctrines that are both religious and aesthetic.[7] These are the doctrines of Analogy and Reserve. Both are closely bound up with typology and figuralism; in fact, from the Tractarian point of view, typology is an aspect of Analogy. Let me summarize each doctrine to make the connections clear.

First, Analogy. This comprehensive Tractarian principle stems above all from John Keble, who first wrote on aesthetic matters as early as 1814, five years before John Ruskin was born. Just as typology finds its first warrant in holy scripture, so too does Analogy. In Romans, St Paul writes: 'The invisible things of [God] from the Creation of the world are clearly seen, being understood by the things that are made.' That is, God so created the world that its very

---

[7] See esp. Stephen Prickett, *Romanticism and Religion: The Tradition of Coleridge and Wordsworth in the Victorian Church* (Cambridge, 1976); G.B. Tennyson, 'The Sacramental Imagination,' in *Nature and the Victorian Imagination*, ed. U.C. Knoepflmacher and G.B. Tennyson (Berkeley and Los Angeles, 1977), pp. 370–90; 'Tractarian Aesthetics: Analogy and Reserve in Keble and Newman,' *Victorian Newsletter*, No. 55 (Spring, 1979), pp. 8–10; and *Victorian Devotional Poetry* (Cambridge, Ma., 1981).

physical nature contains signs of His creation. This doctrine stands behind the nature poetry of Keble and the Tractarians, as anyone who has looked at *The Christian Year* can attest. It is also related to the notion that God ordained laws and rites in the old dispensation so that he could, to paraphrase Milton, 'inform men by types and shadows' of what was to come in the new. The other doctrine of the Tractarians, also originating with Keble but later especially associated with Keble's pupil Isaac Williams, is the doctrine of Reserve. This is the idea that religion is a veiled and secret matter, not immediately revealed to the profane, but intentionally held back, first by God, then by those who have received the fullness of faith. Reserve lends itself not only to reticence in religious matters but also to reverence and then in turn to figuralism and symbolism, so that holy and sacred things may be approached through signs that lead one gradually to greater understanding.

Both of these concepts, Analogy and Reserve, were being preached by Keble in the teens and twenties of the nineteenth century and subsequently by the Tractarians generally in the thirties and forties. When the 'Oxford Undergraduate' who was to write *Modern Painters* was still in fact an undergraduate Keble and Williams were making contributions to the *Tracts for the Times* that securely anchored their theological-aesthetic thinking in scripture and in the writings of the early Church Fathers and hence in typological, symbolic, and figural approaches to religion and literature.

The pertinent Keble Tract is Tract 89, titled 'On the Mysticism of the Early Fathers.'[8] It is a lengthy treatise designed to justify a symbolic, nay an allegorical, method of reading scripture and hence of reading poetry. Keble takes as a key text on this matter the statement of St Irenaeus: 'For there is with God no useless and no empty sign' (p. 149), and he applied it both to the visible world and to the interpretation of Holy Scripture. He argues for a series of symbolic interpretations of the world and of God's word that he calls 'the Poetical, the Moral, and the Mystical' (p. 143), which correspond more or less to the imaginative, the moral, and the theological in modern terms. Keble feels called upon to defend the concept of

[8] *Tracts for the Times*, 6 vols. (London, 1840). Subsequent references to the *Tracts* taken from this edition are incorporated into the text. Another Tractarian source for typological and figural interpretation is Pusey's Tract 81, 'On Eucharistic Sacrifice' and his 'Lectures on Types and Prophecies,' cited by Alf Härdelin in *The Tractarian Understanding of the Eucharist* (Uppsala, 1965), pp. 16–17, 33–5.

typology in scripture as part of the concept of Analogy. One may well ask, against whom was Keble defending the idea of scriptural typology? We shall see.

As with Tractarian Analogy, so with Reserve. Here the most potent voice was that of Keble's pupil Isaac Williams, though doubtless the most potent personal example of the concept for the Tractarians was, in this as in all other things, Keble himself. Williams devoted two of the *Tracts for the Times* (Numbers 80 and 87) to an elucidation of the doctrine of Reserve. As I have noted, this doctrine meant not only a certain reticence but even more a distinct *reverence* in dealing with religious matters. That reverence found expression in the mystery of religion and in a necessary indirection and veiling in dealing with religious topics. It is at the point of indirection and veiling that Reserve joins company with Analogy. Both are means of shadowing forth greater spiritual realities by means of lesser instruments. As the Tractarians found that God had shadowed himself forth in the creation of the visible world, so they could not fail to appreciate that He had done likewise in Scripture by shadowing forth the New Testament through types and figures in the Old. Williams argues in this Tract that, since the ancient Church interpreted scripture as 'being figured and shadowed out by an infinity of types,' so we may conclude that 'God has hid this vastness of Analogy and types in His word and His works.'

Williams's first Tract on Reserve was said to have 'aroused the ire of the Peculiars,' and Williams undertook to rouse it further with the continuation of the Tract in a later number. Now, 'Peculiars' was an Oxford nickname for none other than members of the Evangelical party. With their alleged enthusiasm for typology it would seem more appropriate for the Peculiars to have welcomed Williams as an ally. But the fact is that the Evangelicals, for all the typological zeal attributed to them, disliked anything that smacked of secrecy in worship, or patristics in exegesis. And Williams made it plain that the Tractarian approach to Analogy-Reserve-Typology was deeply involved with both secrecy and patristics, hence with allegory and symbolic readings. So, I must add, is much Victorian typology. Holman Hunt himself, after inspecting the actual painting of Tintoretto's *Annunciation* in Venice in company with Ruskin in 1869, not only confirmed in his mind the symbolic readings Ruskin had offered in *Modern Painters* but went on to offer a justification for such practices in art that reads rather like a Tractarian defence of symbolism in the face of Evangelical objections:

When language [writes Hunt] was not transcendental enough to complete the meaning of a revelation, symbols were relied upon for heavenly teaching, and familiar images, chosen from the known, were made to mirror the unknown spiritual truth. The forerunners and contemporaries of Tintoretto had consecrated the custom, to which he gave a larger value and more original meaning.[9]

Need I emphasize again that Tintoretto's forerunners were far removed from Evangelicalism but not at all removed from mediaeval symbolism and allegory?

So much, then, for the theoretical side of the Tractarian attitude towards matters like typology. We must of course bear in mind that I have cited only a few out of many Tractarian treatises that advance the same general ideas. The practical side of this Tractarian theory surfaces in the poetry of those same Tractarians.

The poetry of the Tractarians, like their theory, is full of the kind of typological allusions that are supposed to be the exclusive property of the Evangelicals. Indeed, High Church and Roman Catholic poetry later in the age is the most frequent source from which modern-day scholars of Victorian typology draw their literary examples, insisting the while that somehow all this, too, came from Evangelical sources. Leaving aside the contortions necessary to evangelicalize such decidedly non-Evangelical poets as Christina Rossetti and Gerard Manley Hopkins, one could perhaps argue that Keble's *The Christian Year* was at least compatible with Evangelical churchmanship. As the most popular volume of religious verse in the age, it certainly did find broad favour. Still, it was generally regarded as the bible of High Church Anglicans, and in any case, Keble's poetry was the work of a man conspicuous for his distance from Evangelical influences. It was Keble, after all, who delivered Newman from the last traces of Newman's early Evangelicalism and introduced him to the sacramental system and the doctrine of Analogy.[10] Yet Keble, the non-Evangelical, was writing poetry in the 1820s with lines like the following in reference to Moses:

---

[9] *Pre-Raphaelitism and the Pre-Raphaelite Brotherhood*, 2 vols. (London, 1905), II, 260–1.
[10] See John Henry Newman, *Apologia pro vita sua*, ed. Martin Svaglic (Oxford, 1967), p. 29.

There one by one his spirit saw
   Of things divine the shadows bright,
The pageant of God's perfect law;
   Yet felt not full delight.
Through gold and gems, a dazzling maze,
   From veil to veil the vision led,
And ended, where unearthly rays
   From o'er the ark were shed.[11]
('Thirteenth Sunday after Trinity')

Keble's verse alone stands as a dragon in the gate for modern proponents of the Evangelical source school of Victorian typology. More challenging, however, to the dominant view on Victorian typology is the poetry of Isaac Williams. Like his treatises on Reserve calculated to offend Evangelicals, Williams's volumes of poetry are so visibly non-Evangelical that no amount of generalization about the impact of Evangelical thought can account for them. Yet those volumes of verse, rich in typological readings, can help account for the way the Victorian age received some of its views of typology, analogy, symbolism, and allegory.

Because Isaac Williams is so little known today, his achievement has been entirely overlooked in the study of Victorian typology. Even in his own age Williams (1802–65) was once called 'Keble's moon,' as though he were but a faint shadow of the greater poet.[12] If that is true at all, it is true only of Williams's first volume of verse, *Thoughts in Past Years* (1838), where the prominence of the analogy of nature inevitably calls to mind the better-known poetry of Keble. In the volumes of poetry written after that time Williams marks out an area distinctly his own. I have referred to Williams's 'volumes of poetry' rather than to Williams's poetry *tout court*, for it is not the poetry alone that makes his work so distinctive. It is the union of poetry with illustrations and external visual devices that brings home the character of Williams's accomplishment.

The volumes of greatest consequence for our concern are: *The Cathedral* (1838), *The Baptistery* (1842), and *The Altar* (1847). I shall concentrate on the first two. *The Cathedral*, published in the same year as Williams's two tracts on the subject of Reserve, sets the tone

[11] Citations from *The Christian Year* are taken from the Walter Lock edition, London, 1895.
[12] For a modern account of Williams's life, see O.W. Jones, *Isaac Williams and His Circle* (London, 1971). For an account of Williams as a poet, see my *Victorian Devotional Poetry*, pp. 138–72.

for what he was to do in succeeding volumes. *The Cathedral* profusely illustrates the various parts of a representative Gothic cathedral with etchings of the corresponding parts of actual English and French cathedrals. The poems in the volume are all designed to illustrate the distinctive architectural features of a typical cathedral and hence the distinctive Christian truths that the cathedral itself is designed to proclaim. Wordsworth had said that he conceived of his own poetry as forming the parts of a Gothic cathedral; Williams actually implemented such a plan with a relentless consistency.[13] [Fig. 2]

Now all of this, one might well argue, is merely broadly symbolic, and symbolic in an essentially mediaeval way, not in a narrowly typological way. But that is part of the point. Typology is but an aspect of a far-reaching symbolism which the Tractarians had no intention of divorcing from its patristic and mediaeval associations. Evangelicals may have so divorced it, but it is far from certain that they succeeded even among their own in making the divorce final. As Alf Härdelin makes clear, typology and allegory are very much bound up with one another, even though there are discernible differences between Calvinist and Catholic approaches and applications. He writes: 'Catholic-minded writers are more ready than "Protestant" Anglicans to accept a mysterious presence of the historic events of salvation in the rites of the church, as well as in the individual Christian. The "sense of presence" of past events, therefore, so characteristic of much Christian poetry, tends to have a different purport and meaning in "Catholic" and in "Protestant" poetry; whereas this sense, in "Catholic" poetry can be understood as an analogy to an "objective" presence in the church, in "Protestant" poetry it is a question more of the psychological effect of a literary device, because, for a Calvinist, "Christ is in heaven and not here".'[14]

---

[13] Isaac Williams, *The Cathedral*, 3rd ed. (Oxford, 1841). For additional examples of the visual aspects of Williams's volumes, see *Victorian Devotional Poetry*, pp. 156–69.

[14] Alf Härdelin, 'Katolskt och kalviniskt i engelsk diktning,' *Kyrkohistorisk Årsskrift* (1982), pp. 145–6. The fuller discussion in Swedish under the subtitle 'Typologi och Allegori,' pp. 139–43, criticizes the superficial character of much modern scholarship on this subject and the tendency to overlook some of the distinctions between Catholic and Calvinist approaches. Härdelin's earlier and valuable study, *The Tractarian Understanding of the Eucharist*, is particularly good on the Tractarian understanding of the sacraments and external forms. See pp. 60–71, 226–34.

As for typology more strictly construed, that too is not wanting among the Tractarians and especially in the poetry of Isaac Williams. Here is what Williams does with his poems for the pillars of the cathedral. First come the poems for the pillars of the nave. These represent the patriarchs and prophets of the Old Dispensation. They are matched by an equal number of poems for the pillars of the choir, each representing the Apostles of the New Testament. And the twelve Old Testament figures and twelve New Testament ones are balanced by twenty-four side windows dedicated to 'Ancient Fathers of the Church'. Here are some of the typical, if I may so phrase it, treatments that Williams gives to the patriarchs and prophets. First, Noah:

> It was the stronger Man, Eve's promised Son,
> Bound Death's strong arm within thee, and put on
> His armour: it was Christ in thee enshrin'd,
> Stretching imploring hands to lost mankind.
> In thee His feet found 'rest' amid the gloom,
> Noah, great name of comfort! Lights illume
> The darkness, where He comes with thee to stay;
> And, on th' horizon's verge, a heavenly ray
> Surrounds thee, while the black baptismal flood
> Seems but to lift thee, in thy solitude,
> Nearer th' aerial hall, to walk among
> The stars of Heaven. . . .   (p. 244)

Then, writing of Abraham:

> Was it in that dread hour that Bethlehem's star
> Gleam'd on thy sorrowing heart, and shew'd afar
> That Coming, which shall light this vale of woe?   (p. 245)

Of Moses Williams writes:

> Thus didst thou shadow forth the Living Word
> Who spoke in thee, and nature knew its Lord.
> Cleft at thy rod was the obedient stone,
> And waters learn'd a sweetness not their own.   (p. 247)

As a final example, some lines from the poem on David:

> . . . From Heaven came down
> Such rays of grace, and, forming a bright crown
> Around thy brow, mark'd Jesse's honour'd stem.
> The morning star of royal Bethlehem.   (p. 249)

Similar sorts of typological and symbolic materials can be found in Williams's *The Baptistery* and *The Altar*. *The Baptistery* is a series of poetic meditations on visual scenes figured as adorning the walls of a baptistery. The illustrations were taken from a fifteenth-century book but were entirely congenial to Williams's own way of thinking, which is symbolic to the point of allegory. Some lines from the initial poem titled 'Prefatory Thoughts,' show how Williams once again sought to justify the use of symbolic and typological images against the criticism of such as the Evangelicals:

> Some from tongue and pen
> Banish all figure, comprehend it not:
> Others read wisdom through similitudes,
> Through medium of external sign and form,
> Their speech by nature rich with images,
> And this, if I with reverence so may speak,
> Is God's own language; yes, that Eastern tongue
> Which He hath chosen to converse with man
> Is form'd of symbols. Is not all His world
> And all His word one speaking parable,
> Speaking to sense of things invisible?
> All things with Him are double, each event
> Doth throw its shadow forward; all His word
> Is a full store of countless images,
> Who knows them best is most Divinely wise.
> . . . .
> All earthly things are poor to speak Divine:
> For what are types that set forth things of God,
> Moses to Jesus, or the Ark to Heaven?
> What is the ruin which on Sodom rains,
> Or armies compassing lost Sion's walls,
> To that great Dooms-day which they harbinger?
> Poor shadows all of dread reality.   (pp. xvi–xvii)

And finally, Williams's *The Altar*, though it is concerned with what its subtitle calls 'The Great Christian Sacrifice,' that is, the Crucifixion, has its own abundance of typological references. The volume is another instance of the symbolic attitude of mind in that Williams undertakes to relate Christ's sacrifice to the order of the Mass which recapitulates it. It reminds us that typology, along with allegory, symbol, and figure, is rooted in the structure of Christian worship itself, a structure that predates not only any supposed Victorian Evangelical revival of typology but Evangelicalism and Protestantism itself.

All of this Tractarian material (and much else not cited) had appeared by the mid-eighteen-forties, the very time that Holman Hunt was supposedly awakening the world of Victorian art and literature to typology from his reading of *Modern Painters*. It will now not come as much of a surprise to learn that at Oxford in the late eighteen-thirties a society was formed as a parallel to the now better-known Cambridge Camden Society. It was called the Oxford Society for Promoting the Study of Gothic Architecture. One of its senior committee members was none other than Isaac Williams. One of its regular members was a then Oxford undergraduate named John Ruskin.[15]

The Tractarians did not intentionally seek to innovate, even though much of what they did proved to be innovative. Had they been persuaded that typology was a peculiar pursuit of the Evangelicals (a peculiar pursuit of the Peculiars, as they would have phrased it), they would have given it no welcome in their theological or aesthetic thinking. But unlike latter-day commentators they recognized typology as an aspect of Analogy and as supremely patristic; they recognized it as a feature of the much honoured Primitive Church. Hence it was a rebuke to Evangelicals and Protestants in general. The Reformation, Hurrell Froude said, was a limb badly set. The Tractarians were prepared to set it right. One of the ways to do so was to restore an understanding of the pre-Reformation habits of mind that included typology and allegory as regular aspects of a Christian perception of the world. Tractarians rightly understood that, even though it may be possible to distinguish typology from allegory, the two are nevertheless part of the same disposition of mind. It is not inaccurate, then, of the OED consistently to use 'symbol' and 'symbolism' as terms to define *typology*, or of the *Oxford Dictionary of the Christian Church* to link typology to allegory.[16] The Tractarians knew these connections were inevitable. Therefore they did not

[15] See James White, *The Cambridge Movement* (Cambridge, 1962), p. 24.
[16] The *Oxford Dictionary of the Christian Church* under the entry 'Types' notes as follows: 'A Christian type differs from an allegory in that the historical reference is not lost sight of. Types are looked upon, however, as having greater significance now than was apparent in their pre-Christian OT context. Typology, with an increasingly allegorical emphasis, was much employed in the early Church, esp. by the Alexandrine Fathers, for whom almost everything in the OT was capable of interpretation by this method' (p. 1382).

suffer from the Evangelical mistake of trying to keep the bathwater of typology while casting out the baby of symbolism and allegory, an approach that also characterizes much modern commentary on Victorian biblical typology, bound as such commentary is in its Evangelical fetters. We, too, need to see biblical typology in the Victorian age as part of a larger, wider, and more varied continuation and reinvigoration of an enduring legacy of Christianity to art. To take but two almost random examples, the continued witness in churches and cathedrals of Tree-of-Jesse windows and the persistence in the Roman liturgy of the Good Friday service with its reading of the Prophecies should serve to remind us that much of the allegorical and typological temper of the age was a survival of a tradition rather than the invention of one. For several decades before Fairbairn lamented that typology was a neglected department of the science of theology, the Tractarians were reaffirming it in its symbolic fulness in their theological and aesthetic speculations and in their own poetry as a *living* part of the tradition of Christianity. It still is.

IV

The Brontës and their Father's Faith

ARTHUR POLLARD

Despite notable exceptions, too much criticism still seems to accept the assumption that finds itself expressed most pithily in G. Elsie Harrison's title of her book in which Wesley is represented as *The Clue to the Brontës* (1948). Wesley, it is argued, was Evangelical, Methodist, and, by contrast with the Calvinistic Whitefield, Arminian; and so, the case proceeds, was Patrick Brontë; and so in turn were his daughters. This argument is far too simple. It ignores, for instance, other possible influences on Patrick; it assumes that his daughters followed in his footsteps; it fails to allow for the changes in Methodism between its founder's death and sixty years later; and it leaves us uneasily to try to make sense of the several critical references to this sect in the writings of the Brontë sisters.

John Wesley exercised a remarkable ministry in Ireland as elsewhere, but so also did George Whitefield: and, though Wesley was indeed a great friend and possible influence on Patrick Brontë's sponsor, Thomas Tighe of Drumgooland, we have to recognize also that there was an independent Evangelical Movement within the established Church of Ireland.[1] Tighe sent Patrick Brontë to Cambridge, to St John's, his own old college, where Brontë's tutor was James Wood, an Evangelical and subsequently Master of the college. More important, however, Cambridge at that time was the place of Charles Simeon, the leader of the Evangelical Movement within the Church of England. Patrick was a sizar, or poor scholar, who needed help and gained it partly by his own efforts, partly by those of others. Among these latter were Wilberforce and Henry Thornton who were approached through an intermediary (Simeon's own protégé), Henry Martyn, later to be numbered among the missionary heroes of the Church.

It is as we read Brontë's scholarship on Simeon that we run into still stranger seas of nonsense and error. Thus John Lock and Canon(!) W.T. Dixon in their biography of Patrick, *A Man of Sorrow* (1965), can write:

[1] R.W. Jackson (Dean of Cashel), 'Some Early Irish Evangelists', *The Churchman* LXXXI (1957), pp. 58–64,

Simeon was wielding great influence over the undergraduates and he learned his Methodism from Wesley's great friend, John Fletcher. He was at that time anxious to win recruits to the Evangelical banner to save them from falling into the Calvinistic clutch of the Countess of Huntingdon's 'Connexion' and to retain a leaven of Methodism within the Church as a balance to the High Churchmen of the Establishment. (p. 13)

There is so much wrong with this that one wonders where to start. We will leave aside the last phrase which suggests that if an Anglican was not Methodist, he must be a High Churchman. We can simply refute the implication that Evangelical meant Methodist and was opposed to Calvinistic. We must deny that Simeon learned his Evangelicalism (which was not Methodism) from John Fletcher. Simeon's conversion was remarkable indeed as being free from any active human agency.[2] If there was such an agency subsequently, it was not Fletcher, but Henry Venn of Yelling (and formerly of Huddersfield). John Walsh in his essay on 'The Origins of the Evangelical Revival' rightly claims that 'the ethos of Anglican Evangelicalism was largely formed by men who owed little or nothing to Methodism, and stood increasingly apart from it'.[3]

When Carus's biography appeared, Ellen Nussey offered it to Charlotte, whose reply seems both to imply the differing sympathies of parent and child and to show that Patrick had made clear his own acquaintance with Simeon at Cambridge: 'Your offer of Simeon's "Life" is a very kind one, and I thank you for it. I dare say papa would like to see the work very much, as he knew Mr Simeon' (3 May 1848).[4]

Two matters must be touched on before we leave Simeon. The first is his treatment of Dissenters, particularly as in succeeding years two things happened to sharpen the division of Dissent and the Establishment; namely, the drift of Methodism into Dissent after Wesley's death and the development of more distinctively authoritarian views of the Church, especially after the inception of the Tractarian Movement in 1833, and, secondly, Simeon's position

---

[2] William Carus, *Memoir of Charles Simeon* (1847), pp. 6–9; also, for various aspects of Simeon's life and doctrine, Michael Hennell and Arthur Pollard eds., *Charles Simeon 1759–1836: Essays Written in Commemoration of his Bi-centenary* (London, 1959).

[3] G.V. Bennett and J.D. Walsh eds., *Essays in Modern English Church History* (London, 1966), p. 136.

[4] T.J. Wise and J.A. Symington eds., *The Brontës: Their Lives, Friendships and Correspondence* (London, 1932), hereafter cited as SHB, vol. II, p. 211.

on the Arminian-Calvinistic controversy. This latter is the more important, and for a fuller treatment of the first I would refer the reader to the second section of my essay on 'The Influence and Significance of Simeon's Work' in the bi-centenary volume mentioned above. Basically, what he was saying is summed up in a single sentence: 'Dissenters I never know; all who live in my parish I reckon of my parish.'

The Arminian-Calvinist controversy between Wesley and Whitefield concerned the question as to who would be saved, Wesley considering that God's offer was open to whoever might accept by faith, Whitefield, following Calvin in a strict view that the elect had been chosen by God for salvation. High Calvinism even went so far as to suggest that there was also a fore-ordination of the damned. Wesley and Whitefield differed further, the latter in accordance with Calvinistic tenets emphasizing the final perseverance of the saints (i.e., that the elect, no matter what, would never finally be lost), whereas Wesley stressed Christian perfection, the need to struggle towards what many would claim was really an unattainable condition. I see no evidence of a belief in Christian perfection in the writings of Patrick Brontë—nor in those of Simeon.

What is more important, though, is the question of Simeon's views on the main issue dividing Wesley and Whitefield. We need first to note that it is not simply a matter of being either Calvinist or Arminian, one or the other. Simeon himself could say: 'Though strongly Calvinistic in some respects, I am as strongly Arminian in others.' (Carus, op. cit., p. 563). He could see the worth of both positions: 'Only let any *pious* person, whether Calvinist or Arminian, examine the language of his prayers. . . . The Calvinist will be confessing the extreme depravity of his nature, together with the liability and proneness to fail; and the Arminian will be glorifying God for all that is good within him, and will commit his soul to God in order that He who has laid the foundations of his own spiritual temple may also finish it.' (Preface to *Horae Homileticae*, 1833, pp. xvi–xvii). It did not need to be an issue, as one of Simeon's most distinguished disciples, Thomas Thomason, said: 'I have always made a point to leave these things; as I think it is productive of evil to dive into intricacies that can never be perfectly cleared.'[5] Simeon's

---

[5] C.A. Hulbert, *A Review of the Origin and History of the Elland Clerical Society* (1868), p. 12; Hulbert also shows Thomason's distinction between 'being blameless in life and conversation' and the perfectionist idea that 'whilst one evil thought remained in the soul, it was not born of God'.

position then was neither Calvinist nor Arminian, but holding the best of both in tension. Unfortunately, the fine balance was disturbed in others, in some even violently so. Such a one was William Carus Wilson, founder of Cowan Bridge School, who was refused orders by the Bishop of Chester because of his Calvinism (Carus, op. cit., pp. 418–20). Simeon wrote to Wilson: 'View me on the Calvinistic side, and I am strong as you could wish ... My views are truly scriptural, and at the same time more calculated to unite men of real piety, than the partial statements of either party.' Ten years later Patrick Brontë, who must surely have known something of Wilson's views, sent his daughters to Wilson's school.

The increasing extremism of the Calvinists induced a reaction, and fourteen years after the Cowan Bridge experience Patrick Brontë demonstrated it in his famous letter to J.C. Franks, enquiring about a curate who must not 'deem it his duty to preach the appalling doctrines of personal Election and Reprobation. As I should consider these decidedly derogatory to the Attributes of God, so also I should be fearful of evil consequences to the hearers from the enforcement of final perseverance as an essential article of belief'. (SHB, I, p. 169) The curate was to come as a result of an £80 per annum grant from the Church Pastoral-Aid Society, founded to support 'distinctly Protestant and Evangelical doctrine and principles.' Irony lies in the fact that the whole succession of the curates from Weightman to Nicholls seem to have been High Churchmen! They certainly set about the Dissenters on the matter of church rates; Weightman, Charlotte recorded, 'delivered a noble, eloquent, high-Church, Apostolical succession discourse' which, though admiring, she considered 'bigoted, intolerant and wholly unjustifiable on the grounds of common sense.' (To Ellen Nussey, 7 April 1840—SHB, I, p. 203) In his self-imposed seclusion at Haworth, Patrick Brontë became less fervently Evangelical and less concerned as the years went by. His own devotion to the Church of England, however, increased under the pressure of Dissent as *The Signs of the Times* (1835) and *A Brief Treatise . . . in Answer to a Tract of Peter Pontifex* (1836) make clear. And his inborn Irish-Protestant hostility to Roman Catholicism never waned.

As we turn to the writings of his daughters then, the questions which must occupy us relate to views on salvation, the Establishment, Dissent, and Roman Catholicism. We will begin with Anne. Her case is the simplest, though it has its own complications. One of these is indicated in Charlotte's introduction to Anne's poems. There she claims—and the evidence of Anne generally would support it—that Anne's 'belief in God did not then bring to her dread, as of a stern Judge, but hope, as in a Creator and Saviour ... a sure and steadfast conviction', but Charlotte began the introduction by referring to mournful evidence that religious feeling had been to her much like what it was to Cowper—Cowper, the ultimate Calvinist mockery, who believed himself chosen inescapably for damnation. Anne addresses a poem 'To Cowper' (10 November 1842) in which she identifies herself with him:

> The language of my inmost heart
> I traced in every line
> *My* sins, *my* sorrows, hopes, and fears,
> Were there—and only mine.

She believes that his soul 'in the bosom of its God/ Has found its home at last', but at the end she must ponder:

> Yet, should thy darkest fears be true,
> If Heaven be so severe,
> That such a soul as thine is lost,—
> Oh! how shall *I* appear?

The same note is found in 'Despondency' (20 December 1841) and 'The Doubter's Prayer' (10 September 1843), whilst in 'A Prayer' she writes, with the final word reminiscent of Cowper's own last terrible poem:

> Not only for the past I grieve,
> The future fills me with dismay;
> Unless Thou hasten to relieve,
> Thy suppliant is a castaway.

Here, however, she moves on into some kind of faith, and in 'Confidence' (1 June 1845), though starting 'Oppressed with sin and woe', she ends with the plea.

> Oh, make me wholly Thine!
> Thy love to me impart,
> And let Thy holy Spirit shine
> For ever on my heart.

Later poems sustain this more cheerful note, though recognizing, as in the long 'Self-Communion' (17 April 1848) and 'The Narrow

Way' (27 April 1848), the need for constant struggle. 'Last Lines' (28 January 1849) shows a fine resignation to God's will in suffering, ending nobly:

> Should death be standing at the gate,
>   Thus should I keep my vow;
> But Lord! whatever be my fate,
>   Oh, let me serve Thee now!

Whatever her ultimate position, there is no doubt of Anne's concern around 1842–4 with the Calvinists. 'A Word to the Elect' (28 May 1843), entitled in the original manuscript 'A Word to the Calvinists', half-puzzled, half-angry, attacks their exclusiveness ('But is it sweet to look around, and view/ Thousands excluded from that happiness?'). She went on, however:

> And oh! there lives within my heart
>   A hope, long nursed by me;
> (And should its cheering ray depart,
>   How dark my soul would be!)

> That 'as in Adam *all* have died,
>   In Christ shall *all* men live';
> And ever round His throne abide,
>   Eternal praise to give.

> That even the wicked shall at last
>   Be fitted for the skies;
> And when their dreadful doom is past,
>   To life and light arise.

She appears to have reacted, as some did in her day, towards universalism, and in so doing she finds herself as much opposed to her father's Arminianism as to any Calvinism. No one was fiercer in his warnings about eternal judgement than Patrick Brontë himself. It figures prominently in such poems as 'The Sabbath Bell', 'The Harper of Erin' and 'The Distress and Relief' where we read:

> I hear the Judge Eternal say,
> 'Hence, from my presence, go, thou cursed, away,—
>   'The fiercest, quenchless fire,
>   'And ever-living worm, a prey.'   (*Collected Works*, p. 93)

Dr Tom Winnifrith in his critique of the Brontës' religion has noted this movement in Anne, and he sees it also in *Agnes Grey* 'if we assume, as seems possible, that this was written over a period of some years'.[6] I do not myself detect any clear universalism in the relevant chapters (10 and 11) of this novel, though they do present a highly informed and subtle portrayal of the whole subject of Evangelical salvation, seen from several angles. First, Anne Brontë contrasts the views of rector and curate. The rector, Hatfield, with his insistence upon 'church discipline, rites and ceremonies, apostolical succession, the duty of reverence and obedience to the clergy, the atrocious criminality of dissent, the absolute necessity of observing all the forms of godliness, the reprehensible presumption of individuals who attempt to think for themselves in matters connected with religion, or to be guided by their own interpretations of Scripture' (c.10), is an old-fashioned High Churchman updated with a mixture of Tractarianism, whereas Weston, the curate, is noted for 'the evangelical truth of his doctrine.' It is possible that Weston is based on Weightman as Anne saw him, though, as I have mentioned, he seems to have been more of a High Churchman than an Evangelical. Secondly, Weston is the means of bringing old Nancy Brown to salvation. Nancy, on the one hand, insists to the rector that her conversion had nothing to do with the Methodists, as he implied; and, on the other, her faith is contrasted with the degenerate Evangelical sanctimonious complacency of another old woman, the grandmother in the household where Agnes is a governess (c.4)—a living with a dead faith. Thirdly and most important, there are the insights into the nature of salvation as Anne sees it. Nancy, reporting her conversation with the Rector, says 'I want to have my sins blotted out, and to feel that they are remembered no more against me, and that the love of God is shed abroad in my heart', a conflation of *Acts* 3:19 (recalling *Isaiah* 44:22) and *Romans* 5:5. The first of these ideas, the expunging of sin, is prominent in Evangelical concepts of salvation. It is what Wesley sums up in the line: 'He breaks the power of cancelled sin' (in 'O for a thousand tongues to sing'). In *Agnes Grey*, however, it is the second idea which receives the stress: 'God is love' from the First Epistle of John is repeatedly quoted, and the main passage on the subject contains the sentence: 'The more of love we have within us, the nearer we are to Him', perhaps too much a stress

---

[6] Tom Winnifrith, *The Brontës and Their Background* (London, 1973), p. 58.

on the ethical rather than the conversion experience to please some Evangelical ears.

If universalism is difficult to find in *Agnes Grey*, it is clear enough in *The Tenant of Wildfell Hall* with its story of Helen and her reckless husband. Before she marries him, her aunt warns her of his present ways and probable end: 'How will it be in the end, when you see yourselves parted for ever; you, perhaps, taken into eternal bliss, and he cast into the lake that burneth with unquenchable fire—there for ever to—', to which Helen promptly replies: 'Not for ever ... "only till he has paid the uttermost farthing"'; and then substantiates her view of purgatorial suffering, followed by ultimate salvation, by a battery of texts from Scripture. (c.20) When Huntingdon dies at the end of his brief licentious course, she reiterates this view.

I need to look at this section of the book more fully, because of an aberration of Dr Winnifrith's, which I must refer to and quote from at some length. He is troubled by this 'belief in purging fires, ... since if Anne really believed that we go through a vale of tears now in order to avoid the torments of purgatory hereafter, she believed a doctrine that makes the virtuous seem selfish and gives the vicious an incentive to sin.' He continues:

> To escape from this danger we can imagine somebody working at a doctrine like that suggested in *Jane Eyre*, whereby men are virtuous not to save their own souls, but to save the souls of the wicked. This theory deals with the objection of selfishness, and keeps the deterrent power of purgatory, since the wicked will be released from their torture only if enough people are virtuous. ... In addition the doctrine is a natural extension of the doctrine of Redemption, much favoured by Mr Brontë, and it provides some rationale for the Last Judgement, normally it would seem an unnecessary refinement on the part of the Almighty, who has already judged most people on their deathbeds ... since it refers to the time when sufficient virtue had been accumulated to make further judgement unnecessary. (p. 61)

Having raised his own objection and suggested his own ingenious solution, Dr Winnifrith can then claim that 'The sufferings of Helen Huntingdon, of Lord Lowborough, ... and even of Mr Hargrave, are all necessary to save Huntingdon's soul.' (p. 62) Dr Winnifrith may be uneasy about the moral implications of the virtuous selfishly living virtuously for their own salvation; I am not impressed by his suggestion that they should be living unselfishly in order to let sinners live as selfishly as they like and then find ultimate salvation. I have heard of vicarious sacrifice, but never from that angle before.

What is more, and for us more relevant, it is difficult, if not impossible, to read *The Tenant* in this way. Let us return to Huntingdon's death-bed and see what Anne Brontë has to say. Huntingdon himself questions the validity of a last-minute repentance and is prepared to accept simple justice; otherwise 'Where's the use of a probationary existence, if a man may spend it as he pleases, just contrary to God's decrees, and then go to heaven with the best?' With direct relevance to Dr Winnifrith's thesis, when Huntingdon wishes that Helen might go before God with him to plead for him, she replies, quoting Scripture: '"No man can deliver his brother, nor make agreement unto God for him" . . . : it cost more to redeem their souls—it cost the blood of an incarnate God, perfect and sinless in himself, to redeem us from the bondage of the evil one:—let him plead for you.' (c.49) This is 'the doctrine of Redemption, much favoured by Mr Brontë', much favoured indeed by all Christians, for it is the foundation of their faith, but not capable of extension, only of subversion by any supposed human activity. Anne may differ from her father, but not in that—only, though it is important, in her universalism after purgatorial cleansing.

Emily might well have been closest of all to her father, had she cared to express herself in explicit Christian terms; but what she really believed in this context, we shall never know and have very little on which to base our guesses. Mary Taylor, in a letter to Mrs Gaskell, recorded that she herself had once answered a question to the effect that her religion was a matter between God and herself, whereupon Emily exclaimed 'That's right' and that, she went on to say, 'was all I ever heard Emily say on religious subjects'. (*Life of Charlotte Brontë*, c.8) The poems provide some evidence, but, putting aside, though not dismissing, Fanny Ratchford's thesis that they are all part of a Gondal saga, it is hard to find any consistency within them. At one moment she seems to go beyond Anne in her universalism:

> If thou hast sinned in this world of care,
> Twas but the dust of thy drear abode—
> Thy soul was pure when it entered here,
> And pure it will go again to God.

> ('A.G.A to A.S', 20 May 1838);

but how can one reconcile 'Vengeance will never torture thee,/ Nor hunt thy soul eternally' ('Far, far away', March 1840) with

> Shut from his Maker's smile
> The accursed man shall be:
> Compassion reigns a little while,
> Revenge eternally
> ('Shed no tears . . .', 26 July 1839) ?

One thing is consistent—the repeated plea for 'a chainless soul/ With courage to endure!' ('Riches I hold . . .', 1 March 1841), so that the claim she makes in her best-known poem, 'No coward soul is mine' (2 January 1846), is characteristic. She rejects as 'Vain ... the thousand creeds/ That move men's heart, unutterably vain/ .../ To waken doubt in one/ Holding so fast by thy infinity.' Her grasp of God transcends in egotistic certainty and self-possession anything that might be considered as orthodoxly Christian:

> O God within my breast,
> Almighty ever-present Deity!
> Life that in me hast rest,
> As I, Undying Life, have power in Thee ...
>
> There is not room for Death,
> Nor atom that his might could render void;
> Thou—Thou art Being and Breath
> And what thou art may never be destroyed.

This dares beyond all conventional piety in its assertion of a fused identity of the soul and God, even though the otherness of God remains.

For this reason I do not think that much profit can be derived from an attempt to apply Christian concepts and categories to *Wuthering Heights*. So far as we may try to posit a relationship, J. Hillis Miller seems right when he suggests that in her 'doctrine of the inevitability of sin Emily Brontë is more like the Calvinistic Methodist, George Whitefield, than like the Arminian Wesley'.[7] He goes on to argue that the only 'two possible acts which man can perform' are both evil, one 'to seek to regain the boundless joy of heaven [in] a false and damnable image of communion, the other to separate himself from other people and from God in the form of worldly prudence, the commercial

---

[7] J. Hillis Miller, *The Disappearance of God* (London, 1963), p. 185.

society of getting and spending.' (p. 186) The latter was the sin of Linton, the former that of Cathy in claiming 'I *am* Heathcliff'. What Miller omits to stress, however, is Cathy's inability to help herself, her lack of freedom, which itself suggests something like Calvinistic determinism; and Heathcliff is, as Charlotte described him, 'a man's shape animated by demon life—a Ghoul—an Afreet.' (1850 Preface) Miller concludes that God has been transformed from the transcendent deity of extreme Protestantism, enforcing in wrath his irrevocable laws, to an immanent God, pervading everything. (p. 211) Miller's title is *The Disappearance of God*; I prefer to think that, for all practical purposes, that is what has happened in *Wuthering Heights*.

Certainly Nelly Dean's conventional faith is not only helpless, but also irrelevant, and the only other character who deliberately projects his alleged Christianity is the hypocritical Calvinistic Nonconformist, Joseph, with his belief in God's particular providence: 'All warks togither for gooid tuh them as is chozzen, and piked aht froo' th' rubbidge.' (c.9) Like the chapel minister, Jabes Branderham, Joseph works by a selective and personally convenient literalism. The same attitude of mind produced those 'mad *Methodist Magazines*, full of miracles and apparitions, of preternatural warnings, ominous dreams and frenzied fanaticism', to which Charlotte referred in *Shirley* (*c*.22), a novel in which she also ridiculed the hysteria of instantaneous conversions in the highly emotional atmosphere of hymn-singing and 'an interval of clamorous prayer, accompanied by fearful groans. A shout of "I've found liberty!" "Doad o' Bill's has fun' liberty!" rung from the chapel, and out all the assembly broke again:

> "What a mercy is this!
> What a heaven of bliss!"' (c.9)

The use of dialect in these references should be noted. It reveals the social change that had occurred in Methodism. No longer was it the well-disciplined and well-served movement of Wesley (though even he in Charlotte's eyes was 'a Reformer and an Agitator'—*Shirley*, c.34) or even the movement that Patrick Brontë knew in his early manhood through his contact with Woodhouse Grove School at Apperley Bridge. It had coarsened and dissipated into sub-sects, with local congregations in the hands of ignorant and pretentious leaders. The Brontë sisters had little time for the Methodism they knew.

Charlotte had little time also for Roman Catholicism. She links the two together, speaking in *Villette* of Polly 'praying like some Catholic or Methodist enthusiast' (c.2) and, in a letter, of Cardinal Wiseman's speaking in a smooth whining manner, just like a canting Methodist preacher. (To her father, 17 June 1851, SHB, III, p. 249.) Patrick's own anti-Catholicism is illustrated in *The Maid of Killarney* where he describes the conversion of an old Catholic woman by the agency of a Presbyterian minister and the Bible and where, also, incidentally, he speaks out against Catholic Emancipation.[8] Charlotte's letter to her father is full of scorn, ridiculing Wiseman's appearance and the 'spirit of the hottest zeal' which she saw as characterizing the whole theatrical performance. Whilst undoubtedly expressing her own feelings, she was also relying on the prejudices of her correspondent, for in her other letters on the subject—to W.S. Williams (9 November 1850: SHB, III. p. 179), for instance, of the house of Smith, Elder, a thoughtful agnostic, and to G.H. Lewes (23 November 1850, SHB, pp. 183–4)—she adopts a more reasonable tone.

She had, of course, seen Roman Catholicism at close quarters, and to this Belgian experience she refers at length in *The Professor* and *Villette*. In the first it is more incidental. The discipline inculcated from an early age led, she felt, to its devotees being 'mentally depraved' so that Sylvie, for instance, 'had been early taught to make the dictates of her own reason and conscience subordinate to the will of her spiritual director.' (c.12) In *Villette* the opposition between this attitude of mind and the individualist Protestant ethic lies at the centre of the book. The conflict between a religion she despises and the man she loves provides Lucy's dilemma. She does not compromise: 'For man's good little was done; for God's glory, less . . . God is not with Rome' (c.36), but she recognizes that 'Whatever Romanism may be, there are good Romanists'. (c.34) Lucy lists for Paul Emanuel her indictment of Rome, and:

> When I had so spoken, so declared my faith, and so widely severed myself from him I addressed—then, at last, came a tone accordant, an echo responsive, one sweet chord of harmony in two conflicting spirits.
>
> 'Whatever say priests or controversialists,' murmured M. Emanuel, 'God is good, and loves all the sincere. Believe, then, what you can; believe it as you can; one prayer, at least, we have in common; I also cry—"O Dieu, sois appaisé envers moi qui suis pécheur!"'(c.36)

[8] *Collected Works,* ed. J. Horsfall Turner (1898), pp. 138f. and p. 146.

But, though we never know for certain, it seems likely that the two are not united in the end. During her stay in Brussels Charlotte had written to Ellen Nussey: 'I consider Methodism, Dissenterism, Quakerism, and the extremes of high and low Churchism foolish but Roman Catholicism beats them all.' (July 1842, SHB, I, p. 287)

The beginning of *Shirley* shows her making fun of 'high ... Churchism' with suggestions of Tractarian leanings towards Roman Catholicism: 'The present successors of the Apostles, disciples of Dr Pusey and tools of the Propaganda, were at that time being hatched under cradle-blankets or undergoing regeneration by nursery-baptism in wash-hand basins.' (c.1) Those present successors included the models for the curates in *Shirley*, Mr Brontë's own assistants, who, as Charlotte recorded in a letter to Ellen Nussey on 26 February 1848 (SHB, II, p. 193), were vastly annoyed at the preferment of the Evangelical Bishop of Chester, J.B. Sumner, to the vacancy at Canterbury. But Charlotte is more occupied with manifestations of 'Low Churchism' both because she knew it better and because it had, as it were, been going longer. In *Shirley* we have her mildly satirical portrait of Matthewson Helstone, the very embodiment of the Church Militant, based on Hammond Roberson of Liversedge; but best-known of all her Evangelical characters are the two parsons in *Jane Eyre*, Brocklehurst, founded on Carus Wilson, and St John Rivers, sometimes identified with Henry Nussey, possibly because he proposed marriage to Charlotte, but surely too dull a dog to prefigure Rivers, for whom Henry Martyn seems a better model.

Brocklehurst provides little of a problem and so much has been written about him and Carus Wilson that it would be superfluous to add more. I do want, however, to emphasize the likeness with St John Rivers, if only to bring out the differences. Dr Winnifrith has argued against Carus Wilson as a possible Calvinist because he did not preach predestination (pp. 38–9). As we have seen, he certainly had been regarded as a Calvinist, and I believe that Charlotte meant Brocklehurst to be so regarded. I have already noted the significance of the word 'castaway' in the context of Calvinism. Let me note it again, when Brocklehurst is publicly rebuking Jane: 'Who would think that the Evil One had already found a servant and agent in her? ... This girl, who might be one of God's own lambs, is a little castaway.' (c.7) I move now to the end of the novel, to St John Rivers's reply to Jane when she refuses him and decides to seek Rochester: 'It remains for me, then ... to remember you in my prayers, and to entreat God for you, in all earnestness, that you may not indeed become a castaway. I had thought I recognized in you one of the chosen. But God sees not as man sees. *His* will be done.' (c.35) Earlier, Charlotte had referred to his 'stern allusions to Calvinistic doctrines' and that he had 'not found that peace of God which passeth all understanding'. (c.30) This sternness—and here I reach my contrast—marks both him and Brocklehurst, though, of course, with different attitudes and results. Again, the language is the same. Brocklehurst, as he imposes his discipline on the girls, declares: 'I have a Master to serve whose kingdom is not of this world' (c.7); Rivers, as he prepares to depart for India, says: 'I am the servant of an infallible Master'. (c.34) Though Rivers is humble, he is no less absolute in his demand, but, by contrast with Brocklehurst, and as Charlotte makes clear in her final paragraphs, the demand was absolute in its extreme upon himself.

The intensity that religious faith exercised in Charlotte's life and work must never be underestimated. She admires Rivers, even if she cannot sympathize with him. She admires Helen Burns who can manifest such Christian passivity in the face of brutal and unjust persecution. She admires her sister Anne's resignation in the face of death (To Margaret Wooler, 24 March 1849, SHB, II, p. 317), adding: 'These things would be too much if Reason, unsupported by Religion—were condemned to bear them alone.' The tender susceptibilities of the serious Christian soul constantly occupy her, and nowhere more sensitively than in the consideration of Caroline Helstone who, despite other suggested identifications such as Ellen Nussey, seems to me to derive something from Anne, as Shirley is said to derive from Emily. Caroline's sympathetic remarks about Cowper and his poem 'The Castaway' (c.12) surely in the context of what I have said about Anne and her spiritual difficulties support my conjecture.

What Anne appeared to be suffering in the early 1840s Charlotte experienced years before. There are two letters of 1836 (SHB, I, pp. 140, 147) to Ellen Nussey which I must quote:

I *do* wish to be better than I am. I pray fervently sometimes to be made so. I have stings of conscience—visitings of remorse— glimpses of Holy, inexpressible things, which formerly I used to be a stranger to. It may all die away, I may be in utter midnight, but I implore a Merciful Redeemer that if this be the real dawn of the Gospel, it may still brighten to perfect day. Do not mistake me, Ellen, do not think I am good, I only wish to be so.

And the other:

> I hope, I trust, I might one day become better, far better, than my
> evil wandering thoughts, my corrupt heart, cold to the spirit, and
> warm to the flesh will now permit me to be. I often plan the
> pleasant life which we might lead together, strengthening each
> other in that power of self-denial, that hallowed and glowing
> devotion which the past saints of God often attained to. My eyes
> fill with tears when I contrast the bliss of such a state brightened
> by hopes of the future with the melancholy state I now live in,
> uncertain that I have ever felt true contrition, wandering in
> thought and deed, longing for holiness which I shall *never, never*
> attain—smitten at times to the heart with the conviction that
> ————'s ghastly Calvinistic doctrines are true—darkened in short
> by the very shadows of Spiritual Death! If Christian perfections be
> necessary to Salvation I shall never be saved, my heart is a real hot
> bed for sinful thoughts and as to practice, when I decide on an
> action, I scarcely remember to look to my Redeemer for direction.

This second passage reminds us that Charlotte reacted not only to
'ghastly Calvinistic doctrines' but also to the impossible demands of
Wesley's insistence on Christian perfection.

By the time she wrote her novels she had reached a more balanced
condition. Her links with her father's faith were broader in interest
than those of Anne and more orthodox than those of Emily, and it is
when she is closest to him in the histories she delineated in *Jane Eyre*
that we can measure best the influence of Evangelicalism upon her,
what she accepted, what she despised and what she adapted. I have
dwelt sufficiently on what she despised. What she accepted was to
place all her characters in a strictly Christian and strongly eschatolog-
ical context. There is always the heavenly hope—Helen Burns's 'I
am going to God' (c.9); Jane's parting from Rochester: 'Trust in God
and yourself. Believe in heaven. Hope to meet again there.' (c.27)
There is the universalism—Helen Burns again: 'I hold another creed,
which no one ever taught me, and which I seldom mention; but in
which I delight, and to which I cling: for it extends hope to all; it
makes Eternity a rest—a mighty home, not a terror and an abyss'
(c.6) or Jane's belief in Rochester's salvation: 'Sure was I of His
efficiency to save what He had made; convinced I grew that neither
earth should perish, nor one of the souls it treasured.' (c.28) Charlotte
felt that Branwell had found 'peace and forgiveness in Heaven' (SHB
II, p. 263), and expressed her sorrow to Margaret Wooler at the

clergy's dislike of universal salvation, adding: 'But surely they are not so unreasonable as to expect me to deny or suppress what I believe the truth'. (14 February 1850, SHB, III, p. 75) There is, finally, Rochester's conversion at the end of the novel: 'I began to see and acknowledge the hand of God in my doom. I began to experience remorse, repentance; the wish for reconcilement to my Maker. I began sometimes to pray . . . I humbly entreat my Redeemer to give me strength to lead henceforth a purer life than I have done hitherto.' (c.36) But this was not enough for some clerical critics. *The Church of England Quarterly Review* thought, to quote Charlotte, that 'Mr Rochester should have been represented as going through the mystic process of "regeneration" before any respectable person could have consented to believe his contrition for his past errors sincere'. (To W.S. Williams, 29 March 1848, SHB, II, p. 200)

Not long before she had written to the same correspondent: 'I love the Church of England'. One can understand why she continues: 'Her ministers, indeed, I do not regard as infallible personages. I have seen too much of them for that', but she also went on to say: 'But to the Establishment with all her faults—the profane Athanasian creed *ex*cluded—I am sincerely attached'. (23 December 1847, SHB, II, p. 166) The criticisms of *Jane Eyre* which I have referred to may explain in part her dissatisfaction with the Church's ministers. They certainly show something that had happened to a lot of Evangelicals—they had hardened and narrowed in their views. Patrick Brontë, though perhaps less intense in his conviction, had not allowed this to happen to himself. The liberality which marked his letter to Franks went broader still in his daughters Anne and Charlotte (Emily we cannot judge). As opposing camps of Tractarians and Protestants arrayed themselves against each other, they were content to remain loyal members of the Church of England, independent of all -isms, demonstrating a generous, love-filled (wider even than Wesley's) interpretation of that vital Christianity which they had received as their father's faith.

(This essay was delivered as a paper at the Australasian Victorian Studies Association Conference at Wellington, New Zealand, in 1977.)

V

Scenic Structure of Judgement in 'Middlemarch'

JAMES R. BENNETT

Felicia Bonaparte has examined George Eliot's 'two different but related standards of action' in the inescapable 'contest between will and destiny': (1) 'whatever cannot be changed must be accepted', and (2) 'the equally necessary effort to do whatever "good sense will show to be attended with a likelihood of success."'[1] But how can these standards be achieved when human beings, because of their profound egotism and ignorance, stubbornly resist both? Eliot's answer is knowledge, inductive knowledge derived from experience and experiment. Humans have reached some inductions as to what is for their good or evil. Individuals can—possibly, slightly—reduce the moral stupidity[2] in which each is born, through two kinds of knowledge: (1) knowledge of the difference between self and world, and (2) knowledge of other subjective centres. Through experience knowledge is possible, and through knowledge change. Individuals who can adjust their desires to the empirical world and its inevitable consequences and who can perceive how all other humans are their own self centres ('an equivalent centre of self')[3] can possibly 'mitigate ... the tragic confrontation which defines human existence',[4] for

---

[1] *Will and Destiny: Morality and Tragedy in George Eliot's Novels* (New York, New York Univ. Press, 1975; Chapter III, 'Knowledge and Morality'), p. 114–15. Bernard Paris similarly argues that the central action of *The Mill on the Floss* arises out of the mutual incompatibility of Maggie and her environment. She must adapt or abide the consequences. 'Toward a Revaluation of George Eliot's *The Mill on the Floss*', *Nineteenth Century Fiction*, 11 (1956), pp. 18–31. Eliot's commitment to empiricism is carefully substantiated in Paris's *Experiments in Life: George Eliot's Quest for Values* (Detroit, Wayne State Univ. Press, 1965).

[2] 'We are all of us born in moral stupidity', the narrator of *Middlemarch* remarks, 'taking the world as an udder to feed our supreme selves', Chap. 21, p. 156, from the Riverside Edition of *Middlemarch*, edited by Gordon Haight (Boston, Houghton Mifflin, 1956). All citations are from this edition.

[3] p. 157.

[4] *Will and Destiny*, p. 115. According to Irène Simon self-centredness is an evil which can be overcome through enlarged sympathies and imagination, the possible products of experiences with life. 'Innocence in the Novels of

themselves as individuals and even perhaps for 'the growing good of the world' ('Finale', p. 613).

Eliot expounds the major and minor premises of this inductive doctrine in letters to Charles Bray, author of *The Philosophy of Necessity: or Law in Mind as in Matter.* In nature and in humans, in natural as in moral reality, causality and consequences heavily condition destiny: 'In the fundamental doctrine of your book—that mind presents itself under the same condition of invariableness of antecedent and consequent as all other phenomena . . . I think you know that I agree.'[5] Individuals who learn to distinguish invariability of sequence from desire and to act upon that knowledge may find relative happiness in life. But one kind of experience is pre-eminently important in this doctrine of consequences, and that is the necessity to recognize other humans as equivalent centres of self: the effect 'I ardently long to produce by my writings, is that those who read them should be better able to *imagine* and to *feel* the pains and the joys of those who differ from themselves in everything but the broad fact of being struggling erring human creatures'.[6]

It is a special forte of the novel, Wayne Booth wrote in *The Rhetoric of Fiction*, to 'give form to moral complexities', through the complicated, unique case.[7] How Eliot gives form to her belief in knowledge as virtue has been the subject of many books and articles. Several critics have shown how Eliot in the lives of her characters made concrete what Bertrand Russell described as 'the true method of Ethics . . . inference from empirically ascertained facts . . . obtained in that moral laboratory' of life.[8] Reva Stump, for example, traces Dorothea's growth in vision over the two-and-a-half year period covered in the novel.[9] Dorothea's search for wholeness, clashing with her own ignorance and egotism, with other people, and with

[5] *The George Eliot Letters*, edited by Gordon S. Haight, 9 vols. (New Haven, Yale Univ. Press, 1954–78), II, 403.

[6] *Letters*, III, 111.

[7] *The Rhetoric of Fiction* (Chicago, Univ. of Chicago Press, 1961), p. 188.

[8] *Autobiography* (Boston, Little, Brown, 1967), p. 253.

[9] *Movement and Vision in George Eliot's Novels* (Seattle, Univ. of Washington Press, 1959).

George Eliot', *English Studies Today*, Second Series (Berne; Trancke, 1961), pp. 197–215. Darrell Mansell, Jr., argues that Eliot's protagonists are tragic in the sense that their emotional natures cause them to struggle in vain against the law that every cause has inexorable effects. 'George Eliot's Conception of Tragedy', *Nineteenth-Century Fiction*, 22 (1967), pp. 155–71.

heavy circumstance, results in her unique case in enlarged understanding of herself relative to the world and to other perceiving centres.[10]

Many methods contribute to the moral laboratory of life in fiction for the examination of the complicated case—all of the devices of anticipation and recollection (imaginal and figurative patterns, verbal and structural analogies, inter-scenic connections) binding the narrative's web. But I want to focus upon an important yet neglected method—the organization of individual scenes. The development of each individual character is built almost entirely by anecdotes in which all elements converge to reveal character through conflict. But because a full discussion of all the scenes in the novel is impossible here, I will examine only the scenes in which we first encounter ten major characters,[11] and the scenes constituting the narrative of one character, Fred Vincy.[12] Fred was chosen because his story is conveniently brief yet illustratively full: he is the only extreme egotist in the novel to reach objectivity about himself and empathy for others.

Two techniques particularly structure the individual scene, to guide our understanding of a character's relative moral stupidity or intelligence at the moment: (1) the thoughts and opinions of other characters, some true, some false, expressed either directly to the character under the microscope or to other characters; and the judgements of the narrator expressed as generalizations, and (2) the deeds, words, and thoughts of the scene's central character. These techniques produce the concentrated conflict characteristic of George Eliot's scenes in *Middlemarch*. By the end of the novel we perceive, certainly, that 'We are all of us born in moral stupidity,

---

[10] Dorothea, limited in her perceptions, misconceiving self and world, is buffeted by experience, until she gradually acquires greater insight into self and world. U.C. Knoepflmacher, *'Middlemarch*: Affirmation Through Compromise', *Laughter and Despair: Readings in Ten Novels of the Victorian Era* (Berkeley, Univ. of California Press, 1971), pp. 168–201. She passes through crises and grows in understanding when she accepts her limited possibilities and widens her life by including other perceiving centres. Martha Curry, *'Middlemarch*: Unity and Diversity', *Barat Review*, 5 (1970), 83–92, 101–3.

[11] The ten characters in the order of their appearance: Dorothea (Chap. 1, pp. 5–11), Casaubon (Chap. 2, pp. 12–17), Will (Chap. 9, pp. 58–61), Lydgate (Chaps. 10 and 11, pp. 67–70), Bulstrode (Chaps. 10 and 13, pp. 66, 91–7), Rosamond (Chap. 11, pp. 70–6), Fred (Chap. 11, pp. 74–6), Mary (Chap. 12, pp. 76–90), Farebrother (Chap. 16, pp. 115, 120–1), Caleb Garth (Chap. 24, pp. 182–6).

[12] Fred Vincy (Chapters: 11–12, 14, 16, 23–7, 32, 35–6, 40, 52, 56–7, 66, 86).

taking the world as an udder to feed our supreme selves'. Most of the characters live and die in this condition (Rosamond, Featherstone, Casaubon). Some become more so (Lydgate). But we also perceive how a few characters, through experiences epitomized in their scenes, have risen, a little, out of that stupidity (Mary, Farebrother, Caleb), and how a few more will rise, a little (Dorothea, Will, Fred).

All of the main characters are introduced partly through the conflicting opinions of other characters. This works in two ways, depending upon whether or not the opinions are expressed directly to the character being judged. Will, for example, is attacked and defended (both mainly erroneously) in his first scene only after his departure (Chap. 9, pp. 58–61). Casaubon can see only his present limitations (Will's lack of steady object, his taking no interest in geognosis); Brooke, who is totally ignorant of Will's history or nature, absurdly fancies Will 'may turn out a Bruce or a Mungo Park ... a Byron, a Chatterton, a Churchill.' Casaubon's derogations also evoke two defences from Dorothea—that Will 'has conscientious scruples' in not seeking a profession (wrong), and that people sometimes 'seem idle and weak because they are growing' (right). In this structure the multiple perspectives are mainly reported to the reader: any overt conflict with Will either has already happened (Will versus Casaubon) or will happen (Will versus Brooke, Will versus Dorothea). A more typical structure—involving contest and confrontation—is illustrated by the opening scenes of Rosamond, Dorothea, and Bulstrode.

We perceive Rosamond initially (pp. 70–6) through the approving eyes of Lydgate (Rosamond's 'true Melodic charm'), Mrs Lemon (Rosamond the 'flower' of her school), and Mrs Vincy (Rosamond's 'sweetest temper'), but we also meet her through a sharp verbal contest with her supercilious brother.

Dorothea's entrance is accompanied with little approval. 'She was usually spoken of as being remarkably clever, but with the addition that her sister Celia had more common sense' (p. 5): 'most men thought her bewitching when she was on horseback' (p. 7), but a potential husband has been deterred by rumours of her extreme piety (Dorothea fervidly praying 'on a brick floor by the side of a sick labourer') (p. 7). The 'rural opinion', disturbed by Dorothea's 'too unusual and striking' eyes, prefers Celia, 'as being so amiable and innocent-looking'. Such an opinion, however, is emphatically challenged by the narrator: 'So much subtler is a human mind than the

outside tissues which make a sort of blazonry or clock-face for it'
(p. 7). There has been some 'alarming hearsay' regarding Dorothea's
'lunatic' behaviour, a judgement as dubious in its disproportion as
Dorothea's feeling that 'the solicitudes of feminine fashion appear an
occupation for Bedlam' (p. 6). It is a complex beginning. But Celia's
direct confrontation with Dorothea strikes Dorothea most tellingly
in this first of many intense dialogues, when Celia accurately pene-
trates Dorothea's tyranny, her 'strong assumption of superiority in
this Puritanic toleration' (which initiates the complex web of
yoke/harness analogies in the novel), and Dorothea's inconsistency
in sentimentally lamenting the hardships of miners as she takes the
beautiful gem (which triggers a 'scorching', 'haughty' reply)
(pp. 10–11).

Bulstrode receives the most elaborate introduction through multiple perspectives. We first glimpse him at the pre-wedding party in
Chap. 10, but his first real scene is in Chap. 13 (pp. 91–4). At the
beginning of this chapter, five views of Bulstrode's voice and
looks—most of them prejudiced in one way or the other—are
brandished rapidly. Three groups do not like him; one group likes
him; Lydgate's opinion is morally neutral. The narrator bristles
wittily here, subverting every opinion except, perhaps, Lydgate's
(pp. 91–2). The remainder of the chapter, through two conversations, expands in great detail and increasing hostility the judgement
of Bulstrode by others—Lydgate's guarded and deferential appraisal
followed by Vincy's defensively harsh and threatening indictments
(pp. 94–7). Vincy accuses him of criminal business practices, of
hypocrisy, of obsession with power, and of tyranny: 'it's this sort of
thing makes a man's name stink', Vincy lashes out. Afterwards
Bulstrode, speaking to Lydgate, feels his supreme self by contrasting
his own 'sacred accountableness' to his opponents' 'worldy opposition' (p. 94).

The minor role of the narrator in the introductory scenes deserves
remarking. Compared to the judgements of others and the deeds,
speech, and thoughts of the character under examination, the narrator's estimations are rare. The introduction of several major
characters—Casaubon, Lydgate, and Farebrother—indicates no
comment whatsoever by the narrator. For other introductions—
Will, Fred, Bulstrode, and Rosamond—narrator comment is
extremely brief. The narrator evaluates Fred's flute playing in only a
sentence concluding his first scene—'a wheezy performance, into
which he threw much ambition and an irrepressible hopefulness'

(p. 76). The two long conversations between Bulstrode and Lydgate and Bulstrode and Vincy include only one direct comment from the narrator: at the end of his argument with Vincy the narrator explains that Bulstrode had anticipated Vincy's violent reaction, because it had happened before, but that he could not restrain his readiness to admonish others (p. 97). Three characters receive emphatic appraisal by the narrator in their opening scenes—Dorothea, Mary, and Caleb. The narrator presents both sides regarding Dorothea. She is 'enamoured of intensity', 'rash' in seeking 'greatness', merely 'theoretic' in pursuing her high goals, and retains 'very childlike ideas about marriage' (p. 7). On the other hand, the narrator corrects the rural belief in Celia's greater wisdom, and describes Dorothea, though partly ironically, as 'not in the least self-admiring'. It is a mixed picture, more negative than positive, perhaps, but suggesting the possibility of growth. Mary and Caleb are established by the narrator as moral norms upon their first appearance. Mary possesses 'shrewdness' and 'satiric bitterness' in the presence of Rosamond, and a face 'Rembrandt would have painted with pleasure', for Mary's 'reigning virtue' is 'honesty, truth-telling fairness': 'she neither tried to create illusions, nor indulged in them for her own behoof'; and she can laugh at herself (p. 84). Caleb receives equally high praise for his idealism regarding the social function of labour; however, he possesses one limitation: he cannot manage money·(p. 185).

By the profusion of contradictory judgements and the intensity of the confrontations we are guided to concentrate on the uniqueness of each case, to become precise, to fine-tune our apprehensions, to look for evidence which will truly measure a character's moral vision.

All character-introducing scenes include actions by which we might begin to test the contradictoriness of opinion. Most of these scenes (most of the scenes of the novel) involve collisions between two or more characters—Dorothea versus Celia, Will versus Casaubon, Bulstrode versus Vincy, Rosamond versus Fred, Fred versus Rosamond, Mary versus Rosamond. In the crucible of these confrontations characters are tested for their knowledge of other subjective beings and of the difference between themselves and the world.

In some cases we are given only a glimpse of a character in action. Casaubon's first speech—a plunge into personal problems, self-pity, and personal irritation—ominously contradicts Dorothea's expectations (Chap. 2, p. 13). She will discover that he does indeed 'live too much with the dead'.[13] He cannot meet Mr Brooke's challenge to talk about Adam Smith or Southey or Wilberforce in this scene, but he can tell Brooke how he arranges documents by pigeonholes.

Other entrances are considerably more circumstantial. Rosamond appears already in combat (Chap. 11). Everyone 'she has ... been used to' she hates, including herself (she won't smile because she hates her dimples). Yearning to be a 'lady', she will not marry a Middlemarch man. Obsessed with the desire 'to be of good family', she is in fact ashamed of her own family (p. 75). She disdains especially both Fred and her mother. She quarrels with her mother's 'vulgar' dictum, preferring the more genteel 'the best of them' over her mother's plebeian 'the pick of them' (her mother one-ups her, though, with 'superior') (p. 73). She treats Fred with contempt for his vulgarity, needles him about Mary, ridicules his flute playing (p. 76). Of all the opening scenes, only Bulstrode's vitriolic dialogue with Vincy surpasses Rosamond's in contentious ignorance and egoism.

The introduction of Mary seems at first similar to theirs (Chap. 12). Her first words conflict with Mrs Waule and ironically set too high a moral tone (quickly to be deflated): 'I dislike hearing scandal too much to wish to repeat it' (p. 79). But in the following barbed conversation with Rosamond (pp. 84–6) we see how firm is her mind yet how flexible her emotions. And we also see, unequivocally, her possession of the kinds of knowledge essential to overcoming egoism and ignorance. To Rosamond's comment that Mary's life is 'wretched', Mary replies: '"No" ... curtly, with a little toss of her head. "I think my life is pleasanter than your Miss Morgan's"'. (The dialogue contains several instances of Mary's factual, realistic self-appraisal: 'You mean *my* beauty', 'I am not magnanimous enough'.) Mary knows how to objectify the world; she knows the differences between herself and others; she understands concrete facts—such as poverty—and their consequences. Rosamond responds: 'Yes; but Miss Morgan is so uninteresting, and not young'. And Mary replies: 'She is interesting to herself, I suppose; and I am not at all sure that everything gets easier as one gets older'. Mary knows also how to

[13] Barbara Hardy in 'The Moment of Disenchantment in George Eliot's Novels', *Review of English Studies*, n. s. 5 (1954), pp. 256–64, explains how in almost all of Eliot's novels there is a crisis of disenchantment marking a stage in metamorphosis, an argument supported by David Carroll in 'An Image of Disenchantment in the Novels of George Eliot', *Review of English Studies*, 11 (1960), pp. 29–41.

non-egoistically subjectify the world—that is, to empathize, to enter
into other subjective states of mind.

That Mary possesses self-knowledge and empathy, her actions
from the very beginning make clear. Yet Mary does not possess 'all
the virtues. Plainness has its peculiar temptations and vices quite as
much as beauty' (p. 83). She has 'honesty, truth-telling fairness', 'she
neither tried to create illusions nor indulged in them for her own
behoof', and she can, when in a good mood, laugh at herself (p. 84).
Yet she had not, at the age of twenty-two, attained 'perfect good
sense and good principle'. In spite of her previous protestations to the
contrary, for egoistic reasons she repeats part of Mrs Waule's slander
of Fred (pp. 85 and 79), and, provoked by Rosamond, she declares,
against her true feelings, that she would not marry Fred 'if he asked
me' (p. 86).

The structure of clashing judgements and conflicting individuals
which informs the introductory scene, persists throughout the
novel. I will illustrate the method in the narrative of Fred Vincy, first
by showing how opinion and action function together in his initial
scene, then by rapidly tracing the pattern of opinions and actions in
subsequent scenes.

Immediately preceding Fred's first appearance, Rosy complains of
his late rising and smelling up the house with red herrings, and
declares she will never marry anyone like Fred (pp. 72–3), while her
mother counters with praise for his cleverness, his equality with 'the
best society at college', his gentlemanly status and behaviour. Fred
plunges into the novel (Chap. 11, p. 73) in the middle of a discussion
by his mother and sister on the levels of quality of men—'the pick',
'the best', 'the most superior'. Status, not merit, is their preoccu-
pation. Fred immediately garbles the discussion by several wild
pronouncements—for example, equating slang with register: 'All
choice of words is slang. It marks a class' (p. 73), and defining 'correct
English' as 'the slang of prigs who write history and essays'. As
Rosamond observes, Fred 'will say anything ... to gain' his point.
This lightly satirical picture of a failed undergraduate is darkened
slightly by Fred's rude behaviour to Pritchard, the servant, and, at
least in retrospect, by his feeble defence of Mary against his mother's
attack. In all of these actions (and there are more) we see a foolish
young man, blinded by his mother's adulation, by his family's
aspiration to gentility, and by his great expectations of

Featherstone's property, living the life, as he imagines it, of the idle rich. Fred, at the beginning, possesses no insight into the world and its inevitable consequences, and no understanding of the inner nature of himself or of others. By his own definition, Fred is the prig, insisting upon his opinions, a clever gentleman only in his mother's indulgent eyes, but in reality selfish, lazy, conceited. The scene concludes with Fred playing his flute with 'a wheezy performance, into which he threw much ambition and irrepressible hopefulness' (p. 76).

The structure of opinions intensifies in subsequent scenes. Shortly before Fred and Rosy arrive at Stone Court (Fred's second scene, Chap. 12), Mrs Waule attacks Fred four times (five if we add Featherstone's explicit rephrasing of her several circumlocutions). Featherstone counterattacks with three insincere defences. As soon as Fred enters, however, Featherstone bullies him with exaggerations of Mrs Waule's allegations. In the meantime, Rosy, in another room with Mary, censures Fred repeatedly—he is 'conceited', 'horrid', 'idle', offensive to his father, refuses to take clerical orders. Mary defends him twice, though agreeing about Fred's unfitness 'to be a clergyman' (p. 85). At the end of the scene, as Fred and Rosy depart, again she criticizes him: he 'ought to be ashamed'. And to all of these slings and arrows, Rosy maliciously repeats Mary's provoked resolution never to marry Fred even if he asked her.

Fred's third scene (Chap. 14, pp. 98–101) opens with Bulstrode's letter in defence of Fred against Featherstone's allegation that Fred borrowed on his expectations. The rest of the scene dramatizes Fred's responding to Featherstone's continued cunning manipulation—false accusations in the preceding scene, the enticements of financial reward in this scene.

Fred's next four major scenes, leading up to the destruction of his hopes for a lifetime of genteel idleness, exhibit him again and again rasped and struck and pierced. In Chap. 14 Mary criticizes Fred in several voices ranging from laughter to scorn. 'It seems to me', Mary declares, for example, 'very miserable not to resolve on some course and act accordingly' (p. 102). And she adds her father's condemnation: 'an idle man ought not to exist, much less, be married' (p. 103).

Chapter 23 enlarges the arena of criticism. Fred fears public opinion, fears being looked down upon (p. 169). His father's hostility has resulted in 'an unprecendented storm at home' (p. 171). And the narrator emphasizes in new language Fred's 'taking the world as an udder' in direct address to the reader: 'You will hardly demand that his confidence should have a basis in external facts; such confidence, we know ... is a comfortable disposition leading us to expect that the wisdom of providence or the folly of our friends, the mysteries of luck or the still greater mystery of our high individual value in the universe, will bring about agreeable issues. ...' (p. 168). But Caleb offers a sympathetic point of view—his fondness for Fred, his trust in him (though up to this point little supported by experience).

Even after the reading of Featherstone's will, the heaviest blow he has yet received, the structure of (mainly negative) opinions continues. In Chap. 36 Fred's father severely condemns his idleness. Fred's mother defends him. But in Chap. 40, the attacking and censuring, the stinging and scorching of Fred begin to diminish. He has begun to accept his lot and has returned to college. Farebrother justifies him to the Garths. Caleb urges forgiveness. In Chap. 52 Farebrother vindicates him to Mary: Fred may not be wise, but he has 'affection and sincerity' (p. 278). Mary expresses her faith in his 'sense' if he can choose the right profession, but she demands that he do 'something worthy' before asking for her in marriage (p. 379). In Chap. 56 Caleb rebukes Fred for his illegible writing (p. 413), but Caleb has resolved to take Fred under his wing by now. And Fred is determined now to be guided by what Mary wants (p. 414). Fred still has much to learn from the opinions of others, but the right direction of his life is in sight.

In Fred's second scene, in which Featherstone accuses him of borrowing on his expectations, Fred squirms with denials and flattery. We observe his mercenary motives, his self-deceiving expectations, his generalizing about foolish people believing falsehoods at the moment he is believing Featherstone's (p. 82), his egoistic self-pity over being such a splendid fellow with 'so poor an outlook' (p. 89). It is not a pretty picture. But for one moment we glimpse something different about Fred break through Featherstone's humiliating imputations and his own egoism. We glimpse Fred's potential capacity to understand that each individual is 'an equivalent centre of self', when he feels 'a little sorry for the unloved, unvenerated old man, who with his dropsical legs looked more than usually pitiable in walking. While giving his arm, he thought that he should not himself like to be an old fellow with his constitution breaking up' (p. 83). But it lasts only an instant, for as the narrator generalizes: 'knowing another soul is not for young gentlemen whose consciousness is chiefly made up of their own wishes'.

From irrepressible hopefulness in the first scene, the end of the second scene leaves Fred deeply anxious. From this point on until Fred's great expectations are smashed, Fred's 'buoyant-hearted' optimism receives blow after blow, as his bite on the 'world as an udder' steadily fails to produce success.

In Fred's third scene (Chap. 14), Featherstone's manipulation of Fred's desperation for money decimates Fred's shred of self-knowledge and damages Fred's loyalty to his father and Mary, whom he cowardly fails to defend against Featherstone's animosity. Then he falls into melodramatic, self-inflating self-pity for being 'cramped' beyond most men, and finally into flattery. He is only 'a little ashamed', at last, for being so mercenary.

The next scene (also in Chap. 14), between Mary and Fred, shows Fred even less prepared to differentiate between himself and the world and to see into the life of another. He deceives himself, appraises himself falsely, offers a bragging rationalization for not passing his exams, and infantilely hints at blowing out his brains if Mary will not marry him. The only thing holding him to any sensible behaviour is his 'dread of breaking his word to Mr Garth' and his 'love for Mary and awe of her opinion' (p. 173), even though the resolution is made with a ridiculous 'sense of heroism'.

After losing two horses in bad bargaining (Chap. 23), Fred feels 'utterly downcast' (Chap. 24, p. 177); but spurred by his regard for the Garths, he resolves to confess his derelict squandering of their money. At this crucial point the narrator signifies the power of the act's origin: 'Even much stronger mortals than Fred Vincy hold half their rectitude in the mind of the being they love best' (p. 178). Then something happens to Fred without which knowledge of others is impossible, although, as Fred's life shows, single experiences of this kind do not mean the transformation of a person from blind to seeing, from egoistic to altruistic. He is hit so hard by Mrs Garth's pain over the loss of her ninety-two pounds that 'for the first time' he felt 'something like a tooth of remorse'. Up to that moment 'his pain in the affair ... had consisted almost entirely in the sense that he must seem dishonourable, and sink in the opinion of the Garths'. But now he must face their inconvenience and injury: 'at this moment he suddenly saw himself as a pitiful rascal who was robbing two women of their savings' (p. 183).

But because Fred is still Fred in spite of this revelation of the pain that others and not only himself can feel, and in spite of all his own painful experiences, when in the next scene (Chap. 25) he confesses the loss of the money to Mary, he falls into the most absurd and even repulsive behaviour of his life. After calling himself several black names he takes it all back by saying, 'You always do make the worst of me, I know' (p. 186). He has not learned much apparently. Then he mutters melodramatically, 'You can never forgive me' (p. 187). Mary's rebuke, 'What does it matter whether I forgive you?' does not shake him, for he immediately makes several foolish proposals, then whines and begs and rationalizes, then blunders grossly in comparing Caleb's financial difficulties to his own, then begs for expression of her love—all the while feeling secretly complacent over his expectations, confident in gaining Mary's love once he has the money.

This complacency reflects the power of his false expectation and its crucial role in blinding Fred to himself, the world, and others. No matter how many times the unique case called Fred is subjected to being pummelled or excused or upheld, not until the reading of the will (Chap. 35) can Fred begin to learn to accept what cannot be changed and to do what might be successful. Only then can Fred act usefully on the experiences he has had, can make some inferences from the scenes of his life which will lead to practical choices, and even then he must have the energetic support of three strong and loving persons—Farebrother, Caleb, and Mary (Chaps. 40, 52, 56–7, 66, 86). Gradually Fred recognizes what the world is like and what he and others are and need and desire. Then the stings and darts, the bruises and blows of life gradually lessen, and he gains 'a solid mutual happiness' with Mary.[14]

Eliot's scenes, constructed mainly out of clashing perspectives and characters in conflict, demonstrate her empirical principles and purposes, and they exemplify Wayne Booth's claim for the novel's special strength in giving form to the moral complexities and Bertrand Russell's identification of circumstantiality and morality: 'it is impossible to judge beforehand what our moral opinions of a fact will be'.[15] For it is in her scenes of irreducibly concrete individuals in

[14] Ian Adam has offered an anti-deterministic reading of the possibilities within humans for conversion and salvation in Eliot's fiction. 'Character and Destiny in George Eliot's Fiction', *Nineteenth Century Fiction*, 20, (1965), 127–43. Fred's emergence from egoism rather stresses the deterministic element in her philosophy and novels.

[15] *Autobiography*, p. 253.

action that moral judgements and maxims are 'checked and enlightened by a perpetual reference to the special circumstances that mark the individual lot'.[16]

In her building blocks of action, her scenes, Eliot makes her judgement of character concrete. Within the carefully controlled conflicts of opinions, actions, and thoughts, she assesses the consequences to individuals of possessing or lacking knowledge of the difference between the self and the world and especially the knowledge of other living beings as equally important to themselves. Victorian fiction was 'an art of mediation', its form 'literally a *via media* whose goal is reconciliation'[17]—individual desire and binding circumstance, egotism and altruism, perceiver and object. 'Art is the nearest thing to life', Eliot wrote; 'it is a mode of amplifying experience and extending our contact with our fellowmen beyond the bounds of our personal lot'.[18] It is a Romantic idea, as Shelley wrote in *The Defence of Poetry*: imagination is 'the great instrument of moral good' because it is 'a going out of our own nature, and an identification of ourselves with the beautiful which exists in thought, action, or person, not our own'. For Eliot, scenes provided the hinged doors opening outward to a recognition of the common humanity and universal life within other unique individuals.

[16] *The Mill on the Floss*, ed. Gordon Haight (New York, 1961), p. 435.

[17] Janice Carlisle, *The Sense of an Audience: Dickens, Thackeray, and George Eliot at Mid-Century* (Athens, Georgia, The Univ. of Georgia Press, 1981), p. 9.

[18] *Essays of George Eliot.* Ed. Thomas Pinney (London, Routledge and Kegan Paul, 1963), p. 271.

VI

Diversions of the DNB

PAT ROGERS

I

The *Dictionary of National Biography* is a late-Victorian institution by origin, and it could not be expected to remain immune from reassessment. First issued in sixty-three quarterly volumes between 1885 and 1900, with a three-volume supplement in 1901, it is most commonly found today in the set of twenty-two volumes published in 1908–9. (This was not a line-by-line reprint.)[1] Since then, seven decennial volumes have appeared, carrying the terminal date (as regards the death of its subjects) down to 1970, the latest instalment having appeared in 1981. There is also an epitome and a compact edition which amalgamates all the entries down to 1960. Despite these addenda and recensions, it would be true to say that the great bulk of the enterprise is to be found in the original set of volumes, and thus remains nineteenth-century in its essential character.

The work postdates several major undertakings on the Continent along the lines of *Die Allgemeine Deutsche Biographie* (not to speak of ventures in the mould of *Biographie Universelle*), and it was not the first attempt of its kind in English. One thinks of such impressive collections as *Biographia Britannica* (1747–66, with an incomplete second version a few years later), and cognate works would include such varied compilations as Fuller's *Worthies* and James Granger's *Biographical History* (1769 and later editions), which formed the original basis for 'grangerizing' or supplying extra illustrations to a text. This is quite apart from the growing number of specialized collections, assembling the lives of actors, clergy, doctors, and other groups. In the nineteenth century, for a long time, a central position was held by Aikin's *General Biography* (1799–1815), on which the endlessly industrious Robert Southey assisted; but no truly definitive, quasi-official compilation yet existed. Incidentally, I have

---

[1] For the bibliographical position concerning reprints, see Laurel Brake, 'Problems in Victorian Biography: the *DNB* and the *DNB* "Walter Pater",' *Modern Language Review*, LXX (1975), 731–42.

almost without thinking of the matter checked several facts in this paragraph by means of a quick reference to the *DNB*—so automatic does such an application now seem.

Not everyone in the later Victorian period could be said to perceive the need for a new and comprehensive aid in this area, clear as that need would appear from our present vantage-point. Thus in 1877 one finds Christopher Wordsworth, in the preface to his *Scholae Academicae*, subtitled 'Some Account of Studies at the English Universities in the Eighteenth Century', offering acknowledgement of his indebtedness to 'Mr Thompson Cooper's *New Biographical Dictionary* (1875), a work of most agreeable comprehensiveness'.[2] But Germanic scholarship was already on the march; it was not just at Lord's that gentlemen were encountering a new challenge from the professionals. Even though the old-style 'man of letters' was at, or near, his apogee—a story which has been so perceptively told by John Gross—there was a recognition among this very class of author that a more substantial reference tool was required. The first editor of *DNB* was, of course, Leslie Stephen and he—amongst much else—was not inappropriately taking a leading share at this same moment in the *English Men of Letters* series. The *EML* books are more or less dead: at least, it is very hard to get students to pick up such musty volumes, although they often contain pertinent ideas not superseded by the passage of a century. But *DNB* has hung on more successfully. There are a number of reasons for this power of survival, when literary and historical scholarship have moved so far and so fast as to make its prospects of continuing life appear utterly remote. Partly it is a matter of the continuing series, which has prolonged the *DNB*'s active life into our own times, and made it a sort of *Who Was Who* for the recent decades. More important, perhaps, is the sheer scale of the enterprise. Outmoded in detail, the work hangs together like a major engineering feat. It is rather like the case of Victorian sewers: obsolete in design, flawed in construction, defective in materials, and now crumbling badly in parts, but still *there*, still a basic part of the infrastructure of our lives, unreplaced and in the near future pretty well irreplaceable.

It is all too easy nowadays to find fault with the *DNB*. This is not just because individual entries are based on obsolete and, as it now seems, incomplete evidence. There are wider questions of cultural

[2] Christopher Wordsworth, *Scholae Academicae* (1877; rptd New York, 1968), p. viii.

perspective and large issues of the criteria for admission: I shall turn to some of these in a moment. Yet one must first recognize the scale of achievement: the massive advance which *DNB* represented on its rather puny forebears. Then there is the sheer benefit of scale—the advantage of having so many gathered together in one place, and the facility for cross-reference which such an olympian scheme allows. The *DNB* has been the model for parallel ventures in other English-speaking countries, notably the USA and the older Commonwealth countries. These ventures embody, by definition, more up-to-date scholarship, and their principles of selection may be more in accord with contemporary notions of who counts historically and who does not. But their basic plan is in each case close to that of the *DNB*, and without its inspiration such time-consuming and expensive operations would probably have been slower to get under way.

Some of the commoner charges levelled against the dictionary relate to shifts of emphasis within historical studies. Not very many of the original contributors were historians in any full sense—some not in any sense at all. In any case, they had been trained and had formed their intellectual allegiances in the mid-Victorian era, sometimes even earlier. Though contemporaries of Maitland, to think of a key figure in J.P. Kenyon's 'History Men', they were for the most part products of the civilization which produced John Richard Green, Henry Maine and J.A. Froude, all of whom died early enough to figure in the original set of volumes. They lived before the era of cliometrics, and at a time when economic history was still very much a poor relation. Ideologically they tended to be members, by broad mental allegiance if no more, of the liberal descent of Victorian thinkers. Many contributors were antiquarians pure and simple, nearer Jonathan Oldbuck in outlook than Ranke, let alone Marx. They would certainly not all have accepted the full Carlylean doctrine of heroism, but most probably felt more at ease with history as the narrative of great individual lives than would many people today.

And then there is the vexed question of who actually made it and who didn't. The 1901 supplement was chiefly designed to bring matters up to date, and to record those who had died during the making of the original volumes: criteria for admission among those who died in the 1890s seem to be set a little low. But there is also evidence of some rethinking, with several personages from earlier dates now deemed worthy of a place. Since that time, there has of course been no real opportunity to plug gaps from past epochs. The *DNB* as we have it, though it makes more or less contemporary judgements on the more or less contemporaries who have recently died, has not been able to perform any further catching-up operation.[3] Thus the principles for admission to the main series are those, at the latest, of the first decade of this century. Among the omissions which now look most peculiar are three diarists: Celia Fiennes, whose journeys had sidled out into the world in 1888 but who was very little known until the edition by Christopher Morris in 1949; James Woodforde; and Francis Kilvert, who were nowhere above the horizon. There are others in this category, and one cannot blame the original compilers for their absence. It is only by chance that Pepys, Evelyn and Aubrey were fully covered: they would probably just have earned a shortish entry without their respective private jottings, though *Brief Lives* had not yet reached general consciousness.

Certain other gaps cannot be explained away so easily. It is obvious that some groups are badly under-represented according to our current system of values. There are far too few working-class figures, but equally too few businessmen, merchants and capitalists. A good example might be Sir John Blunt (1667–1733), a significant power in the land at the time of the 'financial revolution', and chief promoter of the South Sea Bubble. An equally regrettable absentee, though 'businessman' is perhaps not quite the right word this time, is Peter Walter (1664?–1746), attorney, usurer, marriage-broker, land-agent and accomplished crook. It happens that both these men had important links with Alexander Popè,[4] but they would certainly be worth an entry independently of that. One may notice in passing that the epigoni of Johnson are less often conspicuous by absence: Boswell had been so fully internalized by the late Victorian profession of authors that even minor figures from the *Life* tend to be present. True, there is no Oliver Edwards—but that would be asking too much.

Another group plainly under-represented is that of women. I am not sure just what the proportion of female entrants is in the dictionary. The so-called 'Statistical Account of the *DNB*' appended to a volume in 1900 tells us some moderately interesting things, as that there are 195 entrants with the surname Smith, and that P and W rank

---

[3] Corrections have appeared in the *Bulletin of the Institute of Historical Research*, and elsewhere, and have been collected: see also Brake, p. 732.

[4] See Howard Erskine-Hill, *The Social Milieu of Alexander Pope* (New Haven and London, 1975), pp. 103–31, 166–203.

almost equal as the first letter of surnames (1807 and 1797 entries respectively). There is a table showing numbers century by century, and we learn that one in five thousand of those believed to have reached adult age has clambered through the obstacles of history to earn a place. The ratio naturally differs from one century to another: there is a gradual decrease in the ratio until it arrives at one in four thousand for the 1800s. This fact is reported alongside a certain dip (in proportion to the adult population) in the 1700s, which the writer puts down to some levelling off in 'the total of men and women of the Dictionary's level of distinction'.

A spot-check, taken over a random sample in the middle of the alphabet, suggests that women account for no more than three per cent of the entries in the original series. Of these a fair number are taken up by what might be called inherited inclusions, that is members of royal or noble families born to a position of eminence. A casual check on letter L in the most recent supplementary volume (deaths from 1961 to 1970) shows only three women out of 45, a proportion still ridiculously low at under seven per cent. This may be an unreliable sample, but the editor is still coy in disclosing such figures for the volume. In the original set, there may have been rather more excuse: one must also remember that wives can sometimes be found under their husband's name. For Dorothy Osborne, see the paragraph in an eighteen-column entry for Sir William Temple. And as for Jane Carlyle, colour her Thomas.

There has been historically a real difficulty in this area. Female worthies were chronicled by people such as Lucy Aikin, but for a long time the prevailing attitude was that displayed by James Boaden at the start of his *Memoirs of Mrs Siddons* (1827):

Biography but seldom selects its ornaments from the gentler sex. Women are devoted as much by nature as by custom to the domestic duties. Their merits are to be felt in their homes and in their offspring; if the former be well ordered, and the latter well bred, the charm of both may without hesitation be ascribed to the mistress and the mother.

The wide range of male ambition, but rarely tempts the modest reserve of our females ... The display of the beauty and the accomplishment of the sex in a station so exalted [as that of a monarch] has seldom, I think, been viewed with envy:—yet in the walks of literature the female is distinguished with rather unwilling admiration. She who yields to a powerful impulse, and indulges either her fancy or her wit, with difficulty escapes from the reproach of pedantry; and is suspected to resign, for literary distinction, much of her *proper* charm, that graceful modesty, which retires from even praise too vehemently pronounced. She is, therefore, generally contented to abstain from many subjects perfectly suited to her power, and allows to the bolder sex the *mental* ascendancy, which might frequently admit of dispute, and not seldom admits indeed of *no* dispute.[5]

It is worth recalling that these words, though they postdate Mary Wollstonecraft by thirty years, were written a decade before Victoria's accession. They illustrate a real difficulty: for not only were women put in a position where it was hard for them to succeed in the world, but even if they managed to do this, they would not be perceived as having succeeded in a mentionable way. One observes that it is female writers who are specially singled out, and it was in just this area that women were challenging the decorum of silence and docility. It may be that Mrs Siddons made a large advance in creating the possibility of female heroism because the growing 'purity of the stage' (as Boaden, and others like him, saw it) licensed a more expressive female way of life in one branch of culture.

The original editors do not seem to have been unduly concerned about this particular imbalance, though they did worry about the number of scientists (more or less adequate, historically, I think). Clergymen would seem at first sight well represented, including, however—this may be something to do with Leslie Stephen—a very good sprinkling of dissenters. There are some surprisingly unpuritanical choices—gamblers like Tregonwell Frampton, ne'er-do-wells like Dennis O'Kelly, and jockeys like John Scott, to confine oneself to figures of the turf. Early cricket is quite well covered, from the Nyrens to Fuller Pilch and Alfred Mynn, though you look in vain for Silver Billy Beldham and Lumpy Stevens. A nice touch appears in the life of Henry Montagu Butler, of Harrow and Trinity fame: 'Despite delicate health he played in the school cricket eleven.' Tom Brown could do no more.

Perhaps the most interesting discussion to date of the limitations of *DNB* occurs in an essay by Laurel Brake published in 1975. She points first of all to the silent revision of entries in the early editions of the work, and then goes on to discuss the making (and possible re-making) of one specific entry, that for Walter Pater. The entry was

---

[5] James Boaden, *Memoirs of Mrs Siddons* (London, 2nd edn, 1833), I, 1–3.

by Edmund Gosse, and originally appeared in Volume 44 a year after Pater's death, which had taken place in 1894. In the 1909 re-issue, an amended version appeared. Laurel Brake describes some of the censorship which went on, possibly at the instigation of Sidney Lee, who had succeeded Leslie Stephen as editor. She notes the suppression of passages in a source which indicated that Winckelmann served as Pater's 'true prototype' not just as critic but also as homosexual. Dr Brake observes:

> Whoever the censor was, he merely honoured one of the great taboos of Victorian biography. The *DNB* editors encouraged frankness on many subjects, but homosexuality proved an exception.

I do not think we should be too critical on this score. As lately as 1981, the outgoing editor was noting that, at length, 'less reticence' was possible about homosexuality, which would make 'more intelligible the career of E.M. Forster or W. Somerset Maugham.' Indeed: and one must remember that certain varieties of heterosexual activity were equally beyond the pale when the *DNB* first appeared. For documentation of this comment, one could turn to a life of the Ossian poet, James Macpherson, which came out in 1894. There the author alludes darkly to illegitimate children fathered by his subject in the following words: 'Macpherson had various adventures of a kind which is not generally recorded in biographies.' *DNB* was if anything rather unprudish by the standards of the age.[6]

Laurel Brake refers to one account of the *DNB* as a shamefaced defence of the work as a 'minimal authority', and she quotes what seems to her a 'sad claim for a great dictionary.' This ends with the passage:

> Obviously its value diminishes as the years pass, but I think that it will remain an essential work of reference, not only to the ordinary enquirer, but even to the historian and specialist for many years to come.[7]

---

[6] B. Saunders, *The Life and Letters of James Macpherson* (1894), p. 296. Other doubtful areas include the coverage of foreigners active in Britain: Angelica Kauffmann is in, and so too Zuccarelli, Rauzzini (mistakenly described as a tenor) and Bonomi—but others, such as Viotti and Lucien Bonaparte, are not. Courtesans, not surprisingly, are a weak point.

[7] Brake, pp. 732, 740. The quotation is from J.L. Kirby.

I feel that this claim is justified, and that it is not too shameful to have to make reservations on points of detail. Laurel Brake is right to draw attention to the errors and to the (little-known) corrections which have been published. But in practice one does use the dictionary principally as a first point of call—a kind of local court of summary jurisdiction or small claims, rather than a place of final appeal. One has to make allowances for its biases, its limitations and its gaps. But that applies to any work compiled so long ago, and after all it is only what posterity will need to perform in respect of our own contributions to knowledge. What will a society with instant access at home to immense data-banks think of such products of the scholarly steam age as the History of Parliament?

II

So much for what might be called the serious function of the *DNB*. In the second part of this essay, I wish to explore some of the joys of the work as they emerge through regular use. These are glancing pleasures culled from promiscuous reading, and to be frank they do not have much bearing on the large questions of reliability and authority just raised. Like its cousin *OED*, *DNB* makes excellent bedtime reading. Its almost inexhaustible trove of fact, anecdote and comment seems to me an underrated corner among the pleasures of reading, if I may be permitted a phrase so redolent of the 'Vicwardian' era in which *DNB* had its origins. The examples which follow could be multiplied many times over: they have come to my attention whilst I was looking for something else, and presumably more sustained 'research' would yield much more—though I am never quite sure about that. Most of the cases are drawn from figures of the past three centuries, with a high concentration in the eighteenth and nineteenth centuries, where my interests happen to have taken me. To facilitate access, the quotations are taken from the two-volume compact edition, with page numbers of this edition in brackets: this omits the 1961–70 entries, but is otherwise complete.

By no means all the sidelights I have in mind are of a trivial character. Often they illuminate—either the age of which the writer speaks, or the age of the writer himself. One could hardly conceive of a more expressive paragraph than the opening section of John Bailey's life of Alfred Lyttelton, which tells us more than a gallery of Spy cartoons. Lyttelton's charm and physical prowess have become cultural, almost moral attributes: 'His unbounded popularity [at

Eton] and the fact that he was the finest player of his time, of cricket, football, rackets, and fives, made him like a king in the school.' No surprise that when he went to the bar, 'his influence among his fellows was out of all proportion to his practice'. The latent irony in 'out of all proportion' is not deliberate. The whole entry (2763) deserves study, as does Lionel Cust on James 'Athenian' Stuart (2023). Revelatory in a different way is the article on the antiquarian Thomas Wright. This catalogues his literary productions at considerable length, but vouchsafes only a single sentence regarding Wright's private circumstances: 'His civil list pension was revived in 1881 in favour of his widow, a French woman whom he married in early life' (2333). Only after the subject's death does the wife get a look-in.

Some notable contributors can be found on their best form, and that includes Leslie Stephen himself. One recalls that Macaulay wrote some of his most trenchant short biographic studies for an encyclopedia. Rarely was Stephen more sharp or mordant than in some of his dictionary entries. There is a good entry for William Mason, containing this passage:

> Mason was a man of considerable abilities and cultivated tastes, who naturally mistook himself for a poet. He accepted the critical canons of his day, taking Gray and Hurd for his authorities, and his serious attempts at poetry are rather vapid performances, to which his attempt to assimilate Gray's style gives an air of affectation . . . He was a good specimen of the more cultivated clergy of his day. (1343)

This is very much the tone that would be taken over by Bloomsbury, but Stephen's manner seems to me more delicate than either Lytton Strachey or his daughter Virginia generally achieved. The anticlericalism is just held in check by the seeming wish to be fair. Then there is a splendid entry for Bulwer Lytton, which shows Stephen at his most drily amusing:

> . . . in 1836 he also published two large volumes of 'Athens, its Rise and Fall', which he judiciously left incomplete after the appearance of the histories of Grote and Thirlwall . . . He joined Dickens in an enterprise for the amelioration of the position of authors . . . it was opened by a festival (29 July 1865), at which Lytton and Dickens appeared as president and vice-president of the guild. Decayed authors, however, were not forthcoming, and the scheme collapsed. (1264)

Best of all is the remark,

> He produced nothing . . . except a Hebrew drama, which he burnt
> because he could not find actors (he did not think of an audience)
> with a sufficient knowledge of the language.

This manner can be off-putting in discursive contexts, as where
Stephen lambasts the weaker deistical thinkers in *History of English
Thought*: here the point is lightly enough made, and the sense of
comedy not out of place.

It is, though, as a gallery of eccentrics that one of the *DNB*'s chief
claims to literary attention lies. Anyone who doubts it might well
look up the entries for personages such as James Graham, Thomas
Bowdler, John Fothergill, Percival Stockdale, Messenger Monsey,
S.J. Pratt, Henry Bate Dudley, John Gabriel Stedman, John Moore,
Thomas Nugent and many others (all those are selected from a
limited period). The oddity of human behaviour and the range of
caprice are splendidly illustrated. There is the gamester (to put it
kindly), Dennis O'Kelly:

> O'Kelly was additionally famous in his own day as the owner of a
> talking parrot, which whistled the 104th Psalm, and was among
> parrots what Eclipse was among racehorses. (1536)

Of the precious Edward Jerningham, we learn that his tragedy *The
Siege of Berwick* was performed at Covent Garden in 1794. 'On the
first night the heroine died, but on the succeeding representations her
life was spared' (1077). Precocious genius is exemplified by Thomas
Percy junior, nephew of the bishop, who compiled an epic and a
tragedy based on Peruvian annals by the time he was nine years old.
Daines Barrington is reported as saying, 'I asked this wonderful boy
how many books he intended to divide his epic poem into, when he
answered that he could not well bring all his matter into less than
twenty-four' (1641).

Unwanted books are quite a specialism of *DNB* entries. There is
the unlucky Francis Twiss, who fell in love with Mrs Siddons but
had to settle for her sister Fanny. He dedicated to his brother-in-law
John Philip Kemble *A Complete Verbal Index to Shakespeare*. Of this
we are told,

> It was a work of immense labour, but as it gives the word only and not the passage in which it occurs, his labours have been superseded by later concordances. Seven hundred and fifty copies were printed of it, and 542 were destroyed by fire in 1807 (2126)

Sales cannot have been fast, as the book had appeared in 1805. Then there is another O'Kelly, Patrick O'Kelly, granted the needless epithet 'eccentric poet'. His main work, 'The Doneraile Litany', consists of a string of curses on the town and people of Doneraile, Co. Cork, where he had been robbed of his watch and chain. 'On Lady Doneraile replacing his property, he wrote "The Palinode", revoking all the former curses' (1536). No palinode, so far as I am aware, followed the appearance of James Elphinston's *Inglish Orthography epittomized, and Propriety's Pocket Diccionary*—see the entry (633) for further details—or Daniel Webb's deathless work entitled *Some Reasons for thinking the Greek Language was borrowed from the Chinese* (see 2215). The reasons do not appear, but cannot have been compelling enough to divert the course of comparative philology for very long. Then there are the inventors, like John Anderson, who 'sympathised with the French revolution' and devised a cannon which he offered to the National Assembly: they put a model in their hall, we are told, inscribed 'The gift of science to liberty'. After this he invented a means of smuggling French newspapers into Germany by balloon. His principles, it is stated, 'made him unpopular with the other professors' at Glasgow university. Anderson is a good example of a serious scientist caught up in bizarre experimentation (see the entry, not very full however, 32).

The misfortunes of the figures who people *DNB* are legion. Peculiar health problems attend a good many: of the essayist P.G. Hamerton we read that a nervous illness, which incapacitated him from railway travel, forced him to resign from his post as critic on the *Saturday Review* (2426). An implausible passage occurs in the life of Admiral Rodney:

> He suffered much from gout, which, it was said, occasionally affected his intellect, though it did not prevent his writing very clear notes in the margin of his copy of Clerk's 'Essay'. (1796)

Health could be preserved by strange means, too: the clergyman T.S. Whalley did well here. At the age of twenty-five, he was presented to a living in the gentle Tennysonian countryside near Spilsby: but the Bishop of Ely, in consequence of its unhealthy situation in the fens, made it a condition that he should never enter into residence. This stipulation he readily complied with, and ... for more than fifty years the duties were discharged by a curate. (2241)

Whalley moved to the Mendips, and died in France aged eighty-two. 'Of old age', as the *DNB* says without emphasis. A minor consequence of temporary ill health is recorded in the entry for the classical scholar R.C. Jebb. A portrait hangs in the hall of Trinity College, and 'it is a faithful likeness; but the sitter was suffering at the time from hay-fever, and the expression is consequently harassed' (2720). There are a few extraordinary deaths over which I shall not linger: enough merely to mention the genealogist J.C. Brooke, who was crushed to death attempting to get into the pit at the Haymarket Theatre (227)—*out of* one could understand, *into* seems peculiar. And there is poor William Mason once more, who before facing up to Leslie Stephen had a truly melancholy end:

> In 1797 Mason hurt his shin on a Friday in stepping out of his carriage. He was able to officiate in his church at Aston on the following Sunday, but died from the injury on the following Wednesday. (1343)

I do not want to appear to be relishing the story, though one suspects that Stephen did.

Among all these amazing treasures, my favourite line in the entire dictionary occurs in the entry for another man of letters, now rather faded from the renown he once enjoyed. This was Ernest Rhys, founder of Everyman's Library. The contributor tells of his marriage, and states that Rhys and his wife worked together as a team. 'They had three children, one son and two daughters, and three homes, all of them in Hampstead' (2856). There may be weightier matters in *DNB*, and I dare say there will be some future juncture when the work will have lost every shred of authority as an aid to historical inquiry. But may that day be long postponed, for it is a remarkable anthology of human words and actions, and will remain worth reading when the tide of scholarship has washed away its other claims.

VII

Indian Religion in English Literature 1675–1967

MARTIN JARRETT-KERR

I

... the Capitalists drink gin and whisky and air planes but let
Indian brown millions starve ...
And I am King of May, naturally, for I am of Slavic parentage
and a Buddhist Jew
who worships the Sacred Heart of Christ the blue body of
Krishna the straight back of Ram
the beads of Chango the Nigerian singing Shiva Shiva in a
manner which I have invented.[1]

That is Allen Ginsberg, who at public poetry readings makes the
crowd murmur ŌM, ŌM, ŌM with him.

What are the links between that and this (1710)?

The method of this *arcanum* is as follows: They violently strain
their eyeballs inward, half-closing the lids; then, as they sit, they
are in a perpetual action of see-saw making a long humm at proper
periods, and continuing the sound at equal height, choosing their
times in those intermissions, while the preacher is at ebb ...
[Thus] the *Jauguis* or enlightened saints of India, see all their
visions by help of an acquired straining and pressure of the eyes.

Swift almost certainly wrote this part of *A Discourse on the Mechanical
Operations of the Spirit*.[2] The sacred syllable *Ōm* and the *Yogin* are
readily recognizable.

Swift used Bernier's *Travels in Mongolia* (1670–1), and so did
Dryden earlier for his play *Aurung-Zeb, A Tragedy* (1675). It would
be interesting to know how many of Dryden's readers, past and
present, could give Aurungzeb's dates, relative to Dryden. The

---

[1] Allen Ginsberg, 'Kraj Majales' (in *The New Writing in USA*, 1967, p. 20).

[2] Jonathan Swift, 'A Discourse on the Mechanical Operations of the
Spirit', 1710 (Bohn ed., Sect. I, i, pp. 157f.); the *arcanum* is the 'Spiritual
Mechanism' about which Swift was writing.

answer is that Aurungzeb's dates were 1618–1707; as Dryden's dates were 1631–1700, the Indian Emperor outlived Dryden by seven years! François Bernier was a physician who was in India from 1656–69, and observed the civil war and the Mughal court during the first period of Aurungzeb's reign. Like Dryden he pictured the Emperor as a Renaissance hero. E.M. Forster had an equally favourable picture of him. Aziz, the Muslim doctor, is delighted that Mrs Moore and Miss Quested have accepted his invitation to the Marabar caves. He says:

> 'You cannot imagine how you have honoured me. I feel like Emperor Babur' ...
> 'I thought another Emperor is your favourite' (said Miss Quested) '—what my book calls Aurungzebe'.
> 'Alamgir? Oh yes, he was of course the more pious. But Babur—never in his life did he betray a friend.'[3]

Sir William Jones, a hundred and twenty years after Bernier, was more critical: 'Aurungzib [was] ... the bloodiest of assassins and the most avaricious of men'.[4]

Sir William was Judge in Calcutta (1783–94). It is astonishing what he achieved in those ten years, Most outstanding was the *Asiatick Society of Benghal* (1874ff.). Indian studies were then passing from the French to the British: partly, perhaps, because of the suppression of the Jesuits (1773–1814), with their cultural and linguistic expertise. We remember that Dryden, after his conversion to Rome, translated a French life of St Francis Xavier which interestingly discusses whether the 'Japonians', who had never heard of Christ, had any chance of eternal salvation.

Jones was remarkably open-minded for his time. He chose 'Asiatick' for the title of his Society, rather than 'Oriental'—'a word merely relative'.[5] Even in 1973 at a Congress of 'Orientalists' the delegates had to protest that 'Oriental' implies that Europe is the centre of the world: 'For Japan and China, the "Orient" would be the United States'.[6] It was Jones who introduced to Europe Kalidasa's *Sacontala, or the Fatal Ring* (1789), which Goethe admired so much;

---

[3] E.M. Forster, *A Passage to India*, 1924 (Everyman ed., p. 123).
[4] Cited in S.N. Mukherjee, *Sir William Jones* (London, 1968), p. 132.
[5] Mukherjee, *Sir William Jones*, p. 82.
[6] Cited in Walter Buhlmann, *The Coming of the Third Church* (London, 1976), p. 85.

and Jones's assistant, Charles Wilkins, was the first to translate the *Bhagavad Gita*.[7] This probably had the greatest influence on the West. It is a pity that Blake's etching has not survived.

Number X—*The Bramins.*—*A Drawing*

The subject is, Mr Wilkin translating the Geeta; an ideal design, suggested by the first publication of that part of the Hindoo Scriptures translated by Mr Wilkin. I understand that my Costume is incorrect, but in this I plead the authority of the ancients, who often deviated from the Habits to preserve the Manners, as in the instance of Laocoön, who, though a priest, is represented naked.

Blake was interested in a wide variety of 'pagan antiquities'; and there were echoes of the *Gita* and of Indian creation-myths in his writings. (Whether he believed in reincarnation is a disputed point.)[8]

II

From Blake onwards the influence widens, and is part of a general loosening-up. The philological discoveries, by Jones and others, of the affinity between Sanskrit, Greek and Latin coincided with the movement away from eighteenth-century neoclassicism—a revolt against the Age of Reason—towards 'Romanticism'. The idea that the Europeans had migrated from a distant, unknown land fired the imagination of poets and novelists at the turn of the century. It was one of the high priests of the Romantic Movement, Friedrick Schlegel, who coined the term 'Comparative Grammar'.

This newly-opened-up 'Asiatick' world met with a ready, often too credulous, response. It is, however, important to distinguish two different elements within that world which met with different responses at different times (and this would be true also of the non-Indian parts of Asia). These are (A) the 'mythological' or story-telling element; and (B) the more strictly 'religious' or 'spiritual-metaphysical'. It was the former which on the whole

[7] *The Bhagvat-Geeta*, translated with notes by Charles Wilkins, 1785 (facsimile reproduction, London, 1959).

[8] William Blake, *A Descriptive Catalogue*, ed. G. Keynes (London, 1966), p. 583. On Blake's views cf. K. Raine, *Blake and Tradition* (London, 1962), and Piloo Nanavatty, 'Blake and the Indian Creation Myths' in V. da Sola Pinto ed., *The Divine Vision: Studies in the Poetry and Art of William Blake* (London, 1957), pp. 163–82.

most influenced nineteenth-century British writers; but, as we shall see, there are elements of both in their response.

And quite soon we find an interesting divergence in attitudes towards Hinduism as a socio-religious phenomenon, in the work of two literary ladies. They are symptoms of differing interpretations of the accounts percolating through from India to the British book-borrowing public.

Elizabeth Hamilton (1758–1816) was the sister of Charles Hamilton of the East India Company, an early member of the Asiatic Society of Calcutta. Elizabeth helped him on his translation from the Persian of the *Bedays* (Guide) to Muslim Law (1791); and when he died at thirty, she preserved his Indian collection, and wrote a fictional *Translation of the Letters of a Hindoo Rajah* (1796), dedicated to Warren Hastings. This tells of the friendship between Rajah Zaarmilla and a young English officer, Captain Percy. Percy died, but Zaarmilla corresponded with his relations and friends, and finally came to England. From there he writes to an Indian friend, who urges him not to desert his Brahmin faith—for Zaarmilla shows signs of admiration for Christianity. However, his stay is long enough for him to explode the claims that Britain is a Christian country. Elizabeth Hamilton in fact uses his imaginary correspondence to indict English faith and morals, compared with those of the upright Indian. The Rajah's friend points out that, far from the West being Christian,

> the most enlightened philosophers [he names Hume, Boling-broke, Voltaire] of Europe are engaged in extirpating from society all regard for the pernicious doctrines it [the Bible] contains ...

Miss Hamilton uses the letters to describe many central themes of Indian mythology and practice. And what distances her from most liberal-minded Indian-lovers of the time is her admiration for the 'caste system' from which she argues for extreme conservative conclusions.

> The separation of the different Casts is absolute and irreversible; it forms the fundamental principle of their laws and the slightest breach of it never fails to incur universal reprobation. Thus the sources of disquiet which have held most of the empires of the earth in a state of perpetual agitation were unknown to the peaceful children of Brahma. The turbulence of ambition ... envy and

... discontent, were equally unknown to a people, where each individual ... walking in the steps of his fathers, considered it as his primary duty to keep in the situation that he firmly believed to have been marked out for him by the hand of Providence ... The patience evinced by this mild and gentle race under the severest suffering, and the indifference with which they view the approach of death ... may be accounted for from their firm belief in a future state.

Until Islam disturbed their peace,

the happiness enjoyed by the Hindoos ... and preserved without any material interruption through such a mighty period of revolving time, as staggers the belief of the very fluctuating nations of Europe, was at length doomed to see its overthrow affected by the restless fury of ... the imposter of Mecca.[9]

(We shall see this concern with the Indian time-scale echoed by other English writers later.) The Rajah's friend, urging him not to be deceived by English ways, sums it up:

Expect not from Europeans to attain the knowledge of any virtue. How should they be learned that are but of yesterday? Their remotest annals extend but to the trifling period of a few thousand years. ...

A very different reaction is expressed in the work of Sydney Owenson (Lady Morgan) whose *The Missionary* enjoyed a brief esteem (1811). Elizabeth Hamilton was born in Dublin but was pure English; Miss Owenson was Ango-Irish, with a deep sympathy for the Irish (see her *The Wild Irish Girl*, 1806). Her father was Roman Catholic, her mother Protestant and anti-papist. Miss Owenson (later Lady Morgan) wrote *The Missionary* while staying with the Marquis of Abercorn and read it aloud as she wrote it. Lady Abercorn 'yawned dismally' and the Marquis (privately) called it 'the greatest nonsense he had ever heard in his life'. Lord Castlereagh, however, thought highly of it—and so, surprisingly, did Castlereagh's great enemy, Shelley.[10]

---

[9] Elizabeth Hamilton, *Translation of the Letters of a Hindoo Rajah* 1796, 2 vols. pp. xvf., xxif., xxv and Vol. II, Letter no. 21, p. 61.
[10] W.R.D. Adams, *Women of Fashion*, 1878, vol. II, p. 286.

It is an extraordinary gothic novel[11] which conceals beneath its enthusiasm as much ignorance of Catholicism as of Hinduism. The hero is Hilarion, nephew of the Portuguese Archbishop of Lisbon. The latter, who is also Hilarion's guardian, sends him to a Franciscan monastery in 1620. The Portuguese are proud to have an Archbishop's nephew, but he refuses special treatment and becomes an ascetic. Yet beneath his holy aspect lurked temptations:

> He sometimes wildly talked of evil deeds, which crossed his brain; of evil passions which shook his frame; and doubted if the mercy of the Redeemer extended to him, whose sinless life was not a sufficient propitiation for sinful thoughts.

He counters this by becoming a missionary. His Uncle-Guardian got him appointed Papal Legate and he sailed for India. On the boat is a Coadjutor, a Jesuit (alas: for they are the foes of Franciscans.) Hilarion has to discipline his subordinate, and the Jesuit vows vengeance.

Hilarion finds a cold welcome at Goa from the chief Inquisitor (also a Jesuit), so he goes off on his own. In Lahore he learns the language (almost overnight) and proceeds to Cashmire and the remote Indian Caucasus. (Perhaps Shelley got his notion of that region from Lady Morgan.) In Lahore he had met 'The Prophetess and *Brachmachira* of Cashmire, Luxima', a renowned vestal virgin dedicated to Brahma:

> Her perfect form ... seemed like the spirit which descends amidst the shadows of the blessed. Considered as the offspring of Brahma, as a ray of divine excellence ... the Indian drew back as he [Hilarion] approached, lest their very breath should pollute that region of purity her respiration consecrated.

In Cashmire Hilarion finds a suitable grotto, and builds an altar there. (He is alone and appears never to say Mass!) At dawn the sun shines on the crucifix, and

> the heart of the Christian throbbed with an holy rapture, as he observed the ray of consecrated light ... He prostrated himself before the first shrine ever raised to his Redeemer, in the most distant and most idolatrous of the provinces of Hindoostan.

[11] *The Missionary, an Indian Tale* by Miss Owenson, 1811, 3 vols.

He takes his crozier (he is, after all, Papal Legate) and sets forth. At a confluence of the Behat and the Indus he finds a pagan shrine—and before it

> appeared a human form, if human it might be called, which stood so bright and so ethereal ... that it seemed but a transient incorporation of the mists of the morning.

It is, of course, Luxima. The Missionary is enraptured by her beauty but repelled by her paganism. 'Mistaken being!' he cries, as he watches the 'vesper worship' of the 'vestal Priestess of Cashmire'; 'Know you what you do? That profanely you offer to the Created, that which belongs to the Creator only?' They argue; she can hold her own, and she is willing to read his Bible, along with her own 'Shastras'. He makes the startling discovery that *she* thinks *him* an 'infidel'.

For half the book (1½ vols out of 3) they argue theology. She falls (blamelessly) in love with him, and he with her. It is celibate love on both sides: he designs her for a Christian convent. Finally he baptizes her in a stream—and 'Nature stood sole sponsor; the incense which filled the air arose from the bosom of the earth'. He gives her a crucifix, but is now troubled because she continues to wear on her arm 'the mantra or Brahmanical rosary, from which the image of *Camdeo* (God of Love) was suspended'. However, she has been cast off, declared a *Chancalas* (outcast) by her people because she has been seen by a *Frangui* (impure foreigner). So they have to make their way secretly back to Lahore. There he puts her into a Dominican convent. But inquisitors have followed them; Hilarion is sent back to Goa, tried, and condemned to the stake for breach of monastic vows and 'seduction of a neophyte'. A female figure suddenly appears, and rescues him from the pyre, crying 'Beloved, I come—Brahma receive and eternally unite our spirits!' The Hindus, long restive under the Spanish Jesuit yoke, rebel. Hilarion and Luxima are able to escape, and hide in a cave. But she was wounded as she had shielded him at the stake. She finally dies in his arms, saying

> 'If for others thou wilt not live, live at least for thy Luxima ... Preach, not to the Brahmins only, but to the Christians, that the sword of destruction ... between the followers of thy faith and mine, may be for ever sheathed. ... Thou wilt soothe away the stubborn prejudice which separates the mild and patient Hindu

from his species; and thou wilt check the Christian zeal, and bid him follow the sacred lesson of the God he serves, who, for years before the Christian era, has extended his merciful indulgence to the errors of the Hindu's mind . . . I died as Brahmin women die, a Hindu in my feelings and my faith'.

Hilarion buries her and sets off to preach this ecumenical gospel. He is never seen again; but for years there were rumours that

in a sparry cavern, among the hills of Serinagar . . . the grotto of congelations, a foreign hermit lived; and later was found dead before an altar—beside him a small urn, with ashes and a cross stained with blood, and the *dsandum* of an Indian brahmin, on which was inscribed 'Luxima!'

The novel is a farrago of extravagant nonsense. But the author had read widely—Bernier, Anquetil du Perron, Colebrooke, travellers' tales, histories of Hindustan and Hindu mythology, and of course the *Asiatic Society* publications. She shows an intriguing sympathy for, and some understanding of, Vedantist spirituality as expressed by 'Luxima' (*Lakshmi*); and what we should call today the spirit of 'inter-faith dialogue' is exhibited somewhat precociously if confusedly in her book. Shelley's was a somewhat lone voice in his admiration: it received a few tepid and condescending reviews and little more. However, nothing daunted, she 'revised' it (retaining most of its glaring errors) and re-issued it shortly before her death in 1851.

III

We can now move from these contrasting ladies to the main stream of the 'English Romantics'. The French critic, Edgar Quinet (1803–75), went so far as to say that every 'Lake poet' began with an Asiatic poem: Sir William Jones had infected 'tous les poètes lakistes' with 'le fièvre de l'Asie'; and he specified in his notes 'École des lacs—Coleridge—Shelley tout indien—Byron etc'.[12] There is even a reference to '*The Missionary* of Miss Owenson' by Langlois (member of the Asiatic Society and French translator of the Rig-Veda)[13]

---

[12] Cited in R. Raymond Schwab, *La Renaissance Orientale* (Paris, 1950), pp. 70, 210.
[13] Schwab, *La Renaissance Orientale*, p. 112; Schwab does not give the title of Langlois's work.

(a)   *Samuel Taylor Coleridge*

Though first in Quinet's list, and though one would expect Coleridge to be more open than most to 'oriental' influence, in fact he proved resistant to it. He reads Wilkins's translation of the *Bhagavad-Gita* (though he demurred at Wilkins's comparison of the *Gita* with Milton); he had studied other works by Sir William Jones, Thomas Maurice and the rest; and had planned a poem, jointly with Southey, on Mohammed. But in fact he had not much sympathy for Hinduism, and in his later writings he can reach the damning conclusion that

> ... their Pantheism or visible God, God, proved to them, not from, but in and by the evidence of their senses ... in conjunction with the languor of a relaxing climate and the lulling of a deep, sombre, and gigantic vegetation, seems to me a natural result of an imbecile understanding, producing indistinction ... when all hues and outlines melt into a garish mist deeming it unity ...[14]

In short, 'Sir W. Jones, Mr Wilkins, etc, great and good as we know them to be' overrated the merit of works which are difficult for the Westerner to estimate.

In the same passage Coleridge threw out hints which suggest that he might have had more sympathy with Buddhism—if that is what he means by 'Their [the Hindus'] next neighbour of the North, the temple-throned infant of Thibet, with the Himālā behind and the cradle of the Ganges at his feet'.

(b)   *Robert Southey*

It seemed likely that Coleridge left India to Southey, who wasn't interested in or qualified for the metaphysics, but enjoyed the kaleidoscopic mythology. Goethe who has had so much to do with 'le fièvre de l'asie', said that he 'couldn't stomach multi-headed and multi-armed gods'.[15] But Southey seems to have revelled in them. He dealt with Islam in the poem *Thalaba*, based on an Arabian tale. But it is *The Curse of Kehama* that is the test case for poeticizing Indian religion. The review of *Kehama* in the *Quarterly* (probably by Walter Scott and Grosvenor Bedford) praised the poem, in spite of its being based 'upon the Hindoo mythology, the most gigantic, cumbrous

---

[14] J.H. Muirhead, *Coleridge as Philosopher* (London, 1930), pp. 283f.
[15] Schwab, *La Renaissance Orientale*, p. 66.

and extravagant system of idolatry to which temples were ever erected'. (Compare William Wilberforce in the house of Commons, 1815: the Hindu gods were 'absolute monsters of lust, injustice, wickedness and cruelty'.) However, the *Quarterly* reviewers concede that

> the Hindoo religion, of which Europeans know little ... is not only curious, as one of the most ancient existing superstitions, but particularly interesting, as regulating the religious beliefs and moral practices of millions whom treaty or conquest has united to the British empire.

Southey anticipated criticism of his subject matter. In his Preface he admitted that

> the Hindu religion of all false religions is the most monstrous in its fables ... No figures can be imagined more anti-picturesque, and less poetical, than the mythological personages of the Bramins.

And he refers to the 'one hundred hands and numerous heads' of the deities. But he has tried, he says, to conceal the most blatant incongruities and to stress the moral principles of which they are the personifications.

A summary of *Kehama* is almost impossible. Briefly, the young prince Arvalen hopes for the hand of the lovely Kailyal, daughter of Ladurlad. Arvalen is impatient and tries to ravish her, but Ladurlad intervenes and in the fight kills Arvalen. Unfortunately Arvalen is the son of King Kehama, the most powerful Rajah on earth. At the ceremonial pyre of Arvalen Kehama puts a curse on Ladurlad, his killer: a strange curse—it punishes him with unending pain, sleeplessness and inability to die, but, concomitantly, gives him immunity against water, sword, sleep or death. Kailyal is about to be seized, to join her lover in a 'suttee' death, when she grasps the wooden statue of the goddess Mariately, which floats her to safety down the river. Her father joins her—both banished—and together they take flight, with many adventures, some tedious and repetitious, some exciting and cliff-hanging. Ladurlad is ironically protected by the Curse which is supposed to be his penalty. Kailyal is regularly rescued, usually at the last moment, by the handsome, agile Ereenia, one of the 'Glendoveers' (Good Spirits). The ghost of Arvalen appears frequently to attempt revenge upon his killer, aided by a repulsive enchantress, Lorrinite, and her monster-team. Ereenia, with his contacts among the gods, manages to counter most of these attacks. But King Kehama, 'Sovereign Master of the vassal World,/ Sole Rajah, the Omnipotent below', is too powerful even for the major gods (Shiva, Vishnu, Indra, let alone Yama, Lord of Hell). Here, in a finely dramatic scene, Kehama is about to consummate his victory. Finely dramatic, but for Southey's interruption, to read Kehama a little sermon:

> O fool of drunken hope and frantic vice!
> Madman! to seek for power beyond thy scope
>   Of knowledge, and to deem
> Less than Omniscience could suffice
> To wield Omnipotence! O fool, to dream
>   That immortality could be
> Thy meed of evil!

For Kehama is about to drink the beverage of immortality, 'the cup of Amreeta'. What he does not know is that 'on the lips which touch it, even such its quality,/ Good or malignant'. He drinks, and becomes a statue, ever holding up the Golden Throne of Yamen. Yamen can now return to his throne; the beautiful Kailyal drinks the same 'cup of Amreeta', but to her it gives immortal purity, and she can now be joined to the Glendoveer, Ereenia; the Curse on her father is also lifted, and in due course he too will be immortal and join his daughter, 'to part no more'.

This hardly does the poem justice: some of it is ridiculous, some dreary; all is in a pseudo-Spenserian rhetoric with occasional Miltonic pastiche. But some of it is striking, and a few unearthly episodes have a compulsive excitement. (One is reminded, perhaps, of Tolkien's *Lord of the Rings*.) But what of the Indian mythology and religion? Southey had read all the experts, but does not disguise his apologetic purpose. The opening burial service of Arvalen gives him an excuse for a long note on a typical 'anti-missionary', Col. Mark Wilkes. Those opposed to missionary work held, says Southey, that

> none but fools, fanatics and pretenders to humanity, would wish to deprive Hindoo women of the right of burning themselves! 'It may be useful' (says Col. Wilkes) 'to examine the reasonableness of interfering with the most exceptionable of their institutions. It has been thought an abomination ... that a widow should immolate herself on the funeral pyre of her deceased husband. But what judgement should be formed of the Hindoo who ... should *forcibly* pretend to stand between a Christian and the hope of eternal salvation'.

To which Southey replies that 'Suttee' is not in the 'Institutes of Manu'; and that some Brahmins would anyway like to abolish it.

Whenever the material seems questionable or over-indulgent, Southey has a footnote citing authorities. To his account of Kehama's triumphal entry into Padalon, he adds an apology for its flamboyance: 'What is this to the coming of Seeva, as given by Mr Maurice, from the Seeva Purana . . .'; and after an extensive quotation Southey comments, 'Throughout the Hindoo fables there is the constant mistake of bulk for sublimity'.

There are occasional exceptions to this external, unsympathetic use of the Indian material. At his funeral the soul of Arvalen asks his father, Kehama:

> . . . Must I, through my years of wandering,
> Shivering and naked to the elements,
>   In wretchedness await
>   The hour of Yamen's wrath?
> I thought thou wouldst embody me anew,
>   Undying as I am.

To this Southey appends a splendid quotation from the *Gita*:

> The soul is not a thing of which a man may say, it hath been, it is about to be, or is to be hereafter . . . As a man throweth away old garments and putteth on new, even so the soul, having quitted its old mortal frames, entereth into others which are new.

There are two or three similar quotations, from the *Gita*, the *Bhagavat*, and the *Laws of Manu*, which are successfully welded into the poetry. But for the most part Southey tried to get the maximum *frisson* out of the wild supernatural tale; and—what is distressing— even the *Gita* is mostly plundered for its extravagances: its real beauty and depth seems largely to have escaped him.

(c) *Shelley*

In 1809, says Medwin, Southey was Shelley's favourite (he was eighteen). 'He had read *Thalaba* till he almost knew it by heart . . . But he still more doted on *Kehama* . . . "My most favourite poem", he wrote in 1811; and he was still reading both epics aloud in 1814.'[16] It

[16] Stuart Curren, *Shelley's Annus Mirabilis: the Maturing of an Epic Vision* (Huntingdon, California, 1975), p. 212, n. 32.

is more surprising that in 1811 he should note, of Lady Morgan's *The Missionary*, 'Since I have read this book I have read no other. But I have thought strangely'. And later he refers to 'the divine Luxima', her heroine.

For so young a man, Shelley was astonishingly well-read in Eastern lore: he possessed the works of Sir William Jones, had read Thomas Maurice's *Indian Antiquities* and *History of Hindostan*, G.S. Faber's *The Origins of Pagan Idolatry* (Maurice and Faber had been at Shelley's college, University College, Oxford), Francis Wilford, Bernier, Anquetil du Perront ... and the rest. True, in his *A Philosophical View of Reform* he says that 'The Indians have been enslaved and cramped by the most severe and paralysing forms which were ever devised by man'.[17] But this is contradicted by the Indian influences on his poetry. The Indian chronology of the Earth's energies (*Prometheus Unbound*, Act I) may well have dictated Shelley's time-scale. As Stuart Curren says,

(Shelley), vastly expanding the Christian history of six thousand years declares that for 3,000,000 years before the revolt of Prometheus, Jupiter had reigned amid 'the shrieks of slaughter' (I.80) committed by 'men convulsed with fears' (I.76).[18]

Shelley's choice of 'The Indian Caucasus' (North Kashmir, the Hindu Kush) for the opening of *Prometheus Unbound* has geographical and mythological significance which oriental scholarship has revealed to us. The Wild Spirit, in the *Ode to the West Wind*, which 'art moving everywhere/ Destroyer and Preserver' may well have behind it the notion of Siva = Vishnu. There is one striking passage in Lady Morgan's *The Missionary* which may have caught Shelley's eye. It expresses Luxima's spirituality—the sense

that matter has no essence, independent of mental perceptions, and that external sensation would vanish into nothing if the divine energy for a moment subsided; that the soul differs in degree but not in kind from the creative spirit of which it is a particle, and into which it will be finally absorbed; that nothing has a pure and absolute existence, but spirit, and that a passionate and exclusive love of Heaven is that feeling only which offers no illusion to the soul, and secures eternal felicity.[19]

[17] P.B. Shelley, *Works* (Julien edition), vol. VIII, pp. 17f.
[18] Curren, *Shelley's Annus Mirabilis*, p. 41.
[19] *The Missionary*, vol. I, p. 71.

Compare Shelley's 'He is made one with Nature; . . . He is a portion of the loveliness/ Which once he made more lovely'—may there not be a touch of Lady Morgan here in Shelley's *Adonais*? Raymond Schwab, in his great book, *La Renaissance Orientale*, says 'here we find no longer a mere exploitation of the decor (but) a new spiritual climate . . . not merely a matter of the epidermis . . . The echo of vedantism has here brought a touch of life to German metaphysics'.[20]

(d)   *Matthew Arnold*

Neither Wordsworth nor Byron has the metaphysical interests required. But if we move on to Arnold we shall find an early openness to the East. In 1845 Arnold read, among a great many other things, Victor Cousin's *Cours de l'histoire de la philosophie moderne*, lectures given in 1825, which had a long discussion of 'mysticism', including the Vedas, Vedantic and Sankya philosophers, Indian scepticism, the Yoga Sutras, and, above all, the *Gita*. Arnold read Wilkins's translation of the *Gita*. And there is no doubt that it influenced his early poetry, especially 'Resignation' (*c.* 1845)

> Action and suffering though he knew—
> He hath not lived, if he lives so.
> He sees, in some great historical land
> A ruler of the people stand. . . .
> Exults, yet for no moment's space
> Envies the all-regarded place . . .

His friend Clough did not share his enthusiasm: he wrote to Clough (1848) 'I am disappointed the Oriental Wisdom . . . pleased you not. To the Greeks, foolishness'. And later, referring to the 'Oriental poem' (the *Gita*), 'The Indians distinguish between meditation and absorption—and knowledge; and between abandoning practice, and abandoning the fruits of action'. The debate between the two friends continued in 'The World and the Optimist', in which Critias (Clough) asks, 'Why, with these mournful rhymes/ Learned in more languid climes,/ Blame our activity?' The poet (Arnold) replies that Fate has decreed that the world should turn 'life's mighty wheel' but nothing comes of it! Arnold was in the mood for melancholy reflection; his deep sympathy in the following years for Senancour's *Obermann* reflects this:

[20]   Schwab, *La Renaissance Orientale*, p. 211.

I hear thee saying now:
Greater by far than thou are dead;
Strive not! die also thou!

However he himself (Arnold) cannot follow Obermann: 'I in the world must live, but thou,/ Thou melancholy shade . . . Farewell!'

A distant, detached admiration for oriental wisdom remained with him all his life. In his inaugural lecture as Oxford Professor of Poetry (1857) he pays a tribute to the Buddha. As late as *St Paul and Protestantism* (1870) he says that Buddhism has 'the sense of right-eousness . . . (and) even . . . the secret of Jesus'; but adds, significantly, that it lacks 'the sweet reasonableness, the unerring balance, the *epieikeia*' of Christianity. His disenchantment with the East may partly spring from his sorrow at the deaths of his brother, William, and his sister-in-law—she in India, and he on his way back. His letters seem to imply that the East is not a place for the Arnolds. But deeper was the philosophical rejection. Schopenhauer died in 1860, and an article on him appeared later in the *Revue des Deux Mondes* (1870) which Arnold read. It was entitled 'Un Bouddhiste Contem-porain en Allemagne'. Arnold commented that Schopenhauer's pessimism 'is plainly a paradox, and . . . human thought . . . instinc-tively feels it to be absurd. The fact is with Jesus'. He continued to press for the teaching of oriental languages and culture. But that is at the notional level. To an Inspector of Schools 'Conduct was three-quarters of life'. Matthew's sister, Jane, wrote of his first volume of poems (1848):

Dear Matt has a good deal of the Eastern Philosopher about him at present which does not suit the European mind.

She was right. It didn't.[21]

IV

The Aftermath—and some conclusions

Though Matthew Arnold, comparing English education with that on the Continent, believed the latter to be superior in its teaching of

---

[21] For these references, see my 'Arnold versus the Orient—some foot-notes to a disenchantment' in *Comparative Literature Studies* (Urbana, Illinois), vol. II, no. 12 (June 1975), pp. 129–46.

Eastern studies, this was largely a reaction to our insularity. With minor exceptions this was true of English writers generally: their interest in India was a self-interest. René Gérard, in *L'Orient et la Pensée Romantique Allemande* (1963), says that Herder's fascination for India was that it made available a natural religion which 'n'offrait rien à quoi le déiste d'alors ne put suscrire'.[22] Similarly the sharp, perceptive Indian critic, Nirad Chaudhuri, has said that the Western idealists 'wanted something illusion-proof', and that it was easy to find in Hindu metaphysics 'a refuge for the spiritual and moral romanticism of nineteenth-century Europe'.[23]

What is more, Europe had exhausted her themes of epic grandeur: hence Wordsworth's transfer of the epic quest inwards; Coleridge's plans for an epic on 'The Fall of Jerusalem'; Keats's turning to Greek mythology; Peacock to the *Zendavesta*; Southey looking to Arabia and India. Shelley perhaps alone had something like a genuine ability to empathize with the East, though the use of it as a rod for his enemies' backs was not absent from his mind. At its best they all looked for an expansion of a Western self, not a search for the self of the East.

Emerson, in the New World, was serious about Hinduism—but was less enamoured of Buddhism. Sturgis Bigelow actually became a Buddhist, and was angry that a Catholic priest, summoned by him to his death-bed, refused to annihilate his soul.[24] Yeats had his Indian guru; T.S. Eliot thought once of becoming a Buddhist, and of course had studied Sanskrit—his early admiration for Jules Laforgue may have been influenced by Laforgue's self-conscious Buddhism. L.H. Myers was nearer than most English writers to a true understanding of Indian thought and life, though his novel, *The Root and the Flower* (1955), gave him an easier task, for it is based on the cosmopolitan court of Akbar. E.M. Forster, in *A Passage to India* (1924) shows how sympathetic he could be to an Indian Muslim—and how scornful of the Hindu. Nirad Chaudhuri found Forster's novel 'insufferable'; but, perhaps surprisingly, he recommends any Western reader wanting to get a feel of the bucolic Krishna, to read the few lines that Kipling wrote on him in 'The Bridgebuilders.' Chaudhuri cannot understand

---

[22] René Gérard, *L'Orient et la Pensée Romantique Allemande* (Paris, 1963), p. 57.

[23] Nirad Chaudhuri, *The Continent of Circe* (London, 1966), p. 91.

[24] Van Wyck Brooks, *New England: The Indian Summer, 1845–1915* (London, 1940), p. 359.

how an Englishman who had not read Jayadeva, Vidyāpati, Jnānas, or Bovindās, was able to get so near to the quintessence of Vaishnava poetry.[25]

(He has not so much to say about *Kim* but other scholars have testified to the accuracy of Kipling's picture of the Lama.)

But it is the Indian creative writers, rather than the critics (though the two often coincide) who have made the real advance. Indian critics have looked at Western literature with a fresh, detached intelligence. And then the imaginative poets and novelists have followed: Sri Aurobindo with his long poem *Savitri* (1972), of which Professor Narasimhaya (a distinguished critic, sometimes known as 'the F.R. Leavis of India') has said that, though he personally finds it unsympathetic, it is 'perhaps the greatest epic in the English language';[26] R.K. Narayan's Malgudi sequence of novels; and above all Raja Rao in his *Kanthapura* (1938), *The Serpent and the Rope* (1960) and *The Cat and Shakespeare* (1965). These, and many others, have widened the range of literary experience. Edwin Arnold's *The Light of Asia* (subtitled 'the Great Renunciation') (1879) has sometimes been thought a turning-point. It was not great poetry, certainly, but it was perhaps something of a *tour-de-force*. In the period between the puzzled scorn of Swift and the syncretic enthusiasm of Alan Ginsberg there was in fact little real development. We have had to wait for our Eastern visitors to bring a genuine exchange.

[25] Chaudhuri, *The Continent of Circe*, p. 176; also on Forster, pp. 68, 93.

[26] C.D. Narasimhaya, 'Indian Writing in English', *Journal of Commonwealth Literature* (*JCL*), nos. 5 and 6 (July 1968); also 'The Art and Philosophy of Raja Rao', ibid. pp. 16–28; C. Narajan, 'A note on Myth and Ritual in *The Serpent and the Rope*', *JCL* Vol. VIII, no. 1 (June 1972), pp. 45–8.

Notes on contributors

Janet Bately has been Professor of English Language and Medieval Literature at King's College, London, since 1977 and was previously Reader in English at Birkbeck College. She is interested in medieval literature and in literary language of all periods. Publications include an edition of the Old English Orosius and articles on the vocabulary of the Alfredian period, also on the language of Dryden and the work of seventeenth-century lexicographers and grammarians.

Richard Proudfoot is Reader in English Literature at King's College, London, and General Editor of the Malone Society and the Arden Shakespeare. His publications include an edition of *The Two Noble Kinsmen*, and articles and reviews in *Shakespeare Survey* and elsewhere. In 1959 he played Don Armado in *Love's Labour's Lost* at Moray House College of Education, Edinburgh.

G.B. Tennyson is Professor of English at the University of California, Los Angeles. He has published numerous articles and books on Victorian and modern British literature, including *'Sartor' Called 'Resartus'*, *Religion and Modern Literature*, *A Carlyle Reader*, *Nature and the Victorian Imagination* and *Victorian Devotional Poetry*. He has recently resumed the editorship of the journal *Nineteenth-Century Fiction*.

Arthur Pollard is G.F. Grant Professor of English Language and Literature in the University of Hull. His writings have included work on English hymns and sermons, George Crabbe and, more particularly, on various Victorian novelists including books on Elizabeth Gaskell and Anthony Trollope. He also edited the letters of the former in collaboration with Professor J.A.V. Chapple.

James R. Bennett is Professor of English at the University of Arkansas, where he was also co-ordinator of the Humanities Programme from 1975 to 1982. He edited the collection of essays entitled *Prose Style: a Historical Approach through Studies* (1971), and founded the journal *Style: an International Journal of Stylistics* in 1967. During 1968–9 he was Fulbright Lecturer at the University of Skopje, Yugoslavia. He has his Ph.D. from Stanford University.

Pat Rogers is Professor of English at the University of Bristol, President of the British Society for Eighteenth-Century Studies 1982–4 and of the Johnson Society 1982–3. He has recently published articles on Gibbon, Boswell, Horace Walpole, Sterne, Cowper, Fanny Burney and Garrick, and is currently working on Joshua Reynolds, the Bluestockings and the Johnson circle.

The Reverend Martin W.R. Jarrett-Kerr is a member of the Community of the Resurrection, Mirfield. His published books include *D.H. Lawrence and Human Existence* (1951), *François Mauriac* (1954) and *Studies in Literature and Belief* (1954). He has taught at the University of Leeds and has broadcast on radio and television. From 1963 to 1967 he was on the Religious Advisory Panel of the Independent Television Authority.